The Cross or Culture

The Cross or Culture

What Ails United Methodism
and What Inspires
Africa Church Growth

Rev. Dr. Edward F. Grant

VANTAGE PRESS
New York

FIRST EDITION

This book is dedicated to my six-year-old son, Edwin, who this early in his life has come to develop a special love for Africa, its people, its animals, and its simple way of life.

Contents

About the Author   ix
Preface   xi
Acknowledgments   xiii

1. Introduction   1
2. Transforming Mission Visit to Southern Africa   17
3. Deep Spirituality   48
4. The Cross in Conflict with Culture   87

Conclusion   117
Endnotes   123

About The Author

Rev. Dr. Edward F. Grant is pastor of the Westbrook United Methodist Church, Westbrook, Maine. He is a member of the New England Conference of the United Methodist Church and chairs the Africa Task Force in that Conference. He is originally from the country of Guyana in the Caribbean. He and his wife, Edwina, have a six-year-old son, Edwin. Dr. Grant is the author of *The Kingdom Within You.*

Preface

For the past thirty years, the United Methodist Church, the second largest protestant denomination in the country (Southern Baptist Convention is the largest), has consistently lost members, with the result that a membership that in 1968 was 11 million is now 8.6 million. The most recent year (1997) for which statistics are available shows a loss of 42,000 members.

In contrast the Methodist Church as a whole, in particular United Methodism, is experiencing phenomenal growth in Africa. Indeed, global statistics on church growth reveal that Christianity is recording its fastest growth currently on the African continent: "In 1960, nearly 11 percent of the world's Christians were Africans. By 1993 that figure had doubled to 22 percent. Today scholars estimate that about 338 million of Africa's 700 million people are Christians." Between 1980 and 1993, the impressive growth figures for the United Methodist Church in Africa are as follows: Angola grew from 42,000 to 110,000 during this period; Burundi from 6,000 to 42,300; Mozambique from 13,000 to 60,000; Zimbabwe from 19,500 to 62,000; Zaire from 210,000 to 730,000. The astonishing increase for Africa as a whole for this period rose to 1,240,500 from 435,000.

"In the midst of new political developments and the old, overwhelming problems of civil war, hunger and poverty, the Church in Southern Africa remains one of the fastest growing Churches on earth."

The New England Conference (United Methodist Church) and prior to it, the Southern New England Conference, has had for the past twelve years a sister covenant partnership in mission with the Methodist Church of Southern Africa, as a result of which, over the years, there has been an exchange of mission teams and individuals, both lay and clergy between these two sister Methodist denominations. And more recently—1999 Annual Conference—a new covenant mission partnership has been established between the New England Conference and our sister United Methodist Conference in West Angola. For all of us who were privileged to visit our sister Methodist Churches in Southern Africa, either individually or as part of a team, it was a truly transforming experience, one we will always cherish very fondly. They had so little, yet they gave so much. In particular, the quality of the spirituality of our African brothers and sisters, including their fervent courageous faith, their triumphant hope, their joyful, enthusiastic spirit, in spite of oppressive poverty and suffering, and their deep sacrificial love and commitment for their Lord and their Church was a powerful inspiration to us all and also a convincing revelation of why the Church in Africa is growing so rapidly and why the United Methodist Church in this country is in continuous and seemingly irreversible numerical decline.

Acknowledgments

A word of thanks to Elizabeth D'Entremont and Junie Dugas for doing such a competent and commendable job of typing the manuscript; and to our Methodist brothers and sisters in Southern Africa whom we were privileged to visit on different occasions for making those visits such transforming and unforgettable experiences of Christian love, joy, and faith.

The Cross or Culture

1

Introduction

The global mission of the Church is the primary mission of the Church. This is the universal message of hope and love that Christ triumphantly proclaimed to His first disciples on His resurrection both as a challenge and a mandate: "All authority in heaven and on earth has been given to me. Go therefore and make disciples of all nations, baptizing them in the name of the Father and of the Son and of the Holy Spirit, and teaching them to obey everything that I have commanded you. And remember, I am with you always, to the end of the age," (Matthew 28:18–20). This biblical mandate is what inspired and challenged the founder and father of Methodism, John Wesley, to claim somewhat arrogantly but most ambitiously and accurately: "The world is my parish." Two centuries and some seventy Methodist denominations after, a worldwide Methodist family of about 30 million Christians constitutes convincing proof that Wesley's bold, biblical, evangelistic claim was no idle, empty boast.

Disciplined and dedicated Methodists of countless cultures, languages, and races around the globe, in the inspired and inspiring tradition, standard and example of the founder of their Church, and motivated by a passion for global mission, have over these past two centuries succeeded in making Methodism a beacon light of Christian hope, love, and peace throughout the world. With such an impressive global Wesleyan witness and influence, one can safely say that Wesley did indeed succeed, with incredible results, in making the world his parish.

Wesley's ardent evangelistic efforts in fully carrying out this divine mandate were attended with such great global success during his life and ministry and in subsequent generations of Methodists, primarily because for him, the divine mandate was in fact a mandate, not an option. Wesley's faith was rooted in the absolute commitment and conviction that "Jesus is Lord!" As a dutiful disciple of his Lord and as a diligent and dedicated servant of his Master therefore, Wesley concluded that the imperative word of the Lord had to be obeyed unquestioningly and without compromise. The disciple does not have and therefore cannot exercise the right or option to change or modify, amend, or alter what is in fact the authentic word of the Lord. And the word of the Lord, however it may be expressed, is always for Wesley an imperative word. Thus the only response of the servant or disciple is to obey—to do, that is, the will and word of the Lord: "Why do you call me 'Lord, Lord,' and do not do what I tell you?" (Luke 6:46). "Not everyone who says to Me, 'Lord, Lord,' will enter the Kingdom of Heaven, but only the one who does the will of my Father in Heaven" (Matthew 7:21).

Those denominations and churches, within and without the global Methodist family, that have experienced and are experiencing exciting, even phenomenal, growth, like those in Africa, are denominations and Churches that have embraced evangelism in both word and deed as an absolute first priority for the Church and that consequently see evangelism as Wesley did, not as a permissible and an incidental option, but as an unconditional mandate, divinely given by the Lord of the Church Himself. On the other hand, denominations and churches, like the United Methodist Church, in this country that have not experienced and are not experiencing growth, but on the contrary show consistent numerical decline from year to year, are those in which evangelism does not truly occupy center stage as the primary driving force of the Church's mission and ministry.

There may in fact be evangelism in those declining denominations and churches, but for the most part, it is an evangelism of word, not of deed. It is an evangelism on the periphery and on the margin of the church's program and mission and not at its heart and center. Indeed in some churches there is not even evangelism in word—there is no evangelism committee and the word "evangelism" is seldom if ever heard in leadership circles in discussion of church plans and programs. And needless to say if the leaders are unwilling or uninterested in leading the church in the only direction that guarantees growth, vision, and vitality, the direction of evangelism, the members or the church as a whole cannot follow. A church whose primary mission does not focus on evangelism in one form or another, and in practical deeds more than pious words, has the perfect prescription for its own demise.

What the Lord of the Church has given as the central and primary mission of the Church cannot and must not be regarded by His servants as incidental, optional, or even irrelevant. It is the Lord alone who is duly and divinely qualified and authorized to define the mission and nature of His Church. We as His servants and disciples have in essence only one duty—to obey the will, word, and command of the Lord. We are faithful to our call to ministry only to the degree that we fully and uncompromisingly carry out the mission of the Church as Christ, the Lord of the Church, defined and determined it.

He has not delegated to us the authority to redefine the mission and purpose of the Church. His only wish and will for us is that we dutifully do what He has commanded. This again is the whole point of His asking His disciples, clearly and candidly and in utter frustration, obviously: "Why do you call me Lord, Lord and do not do what I tell you?" (Luke 6:46). Thus it is not for any church that bears the name of Christ to decide whether or not it will do evangelism. That has already been decided by the Lord Himself. The Church's task in this regard is not a legislative one but only an executive one. What it has to decide is not whether it will do evangelism but how it will do evangelism.

Jesus expressed this absolute first priority of the global mission of the Church in these concise and convincing terms: "But strive first for the Kingdom of God and his righteousness and all these things will be given to you as well" (Matthew 6:33). To strive for God's Kingdom is essentially and emphatically to work for its growth and development in all respects here on earth. And we can only adequately fulfill this first order of the Kingdom's business as decreed by Christ through evangelism. Indeed it is always the case in the spiritual realm, as in any and every other, that once we put first things first, all other things automatically and inevitably fall into their rightful places, for one's own betterment and the progressive good of the cause in question.

When evangelism becomes the first priority of the Church and assumes a central role in our mission as Christians, positive results almost always accompany our efforts, for then the good seed of the word, sown by us in the manner and in the order prescribed by Christ, qualifies for and receives His blessings in that it bears significant fruit: "Other seeds fell on good soil and brought forth grain, some a hundred fold, some sixty, some thirty" (Matthew 13:8). And as Paul so rightly reminds us in the final analysis, it is God who gives the growth and obviously He gives the growth only when we do it in accordance with His will, way and word. "What then is Apollos? What is Paul? Servants through whom you came to believe as the Lord assigned to each. I planted, Apollos watered, but God gave the growth. So neither the one who plants nor the one who waters is anything but only God who gives the growth. The one who plants and the one who waters have a common purpose, and each will receive wages according to the labor of each. For we are God's servants, working together; you are God's field, God's building" (1 Corinthians 3:5–9).

Those of us who participated in the mission exchange visits in Southern Africa as part of the covenant mission partnership between our United Methodist Conference (New England) and the Methodist Church of Southern Africa were deeply impressed with what a pivotal and prominent place the Word of God genuinely occupied in their lives and in their churches. Indeed there was clearly a radical contrast between how United Methodists here really regard the word of God and how they did. To them the word of God is indeed sacred. But it begins at the very fundamental point at which it began for Wesley—their relationship with Christ.

For them, like Wesley, Christ is indeed Lord. And He is Lord in deed more than in word. And like Wesley, because Christ is Lord, His word is a command not a request. It is an imperative word, not an indicative word. The servant or disciple does not have the option whether or not to obey the Master's word, for obeying the word of the Master is essentially what being a disciple is all about: "While he was saying this, a woman in the crowd raised her voice and said to him, 'Blessed is the womb that bore you and the breasts that nursed you.' But He said, 'Blessed rather are those who hear the word of God and obey it' " (Luke 11:27–28).

And the inspiring story that the devoted, dedicated, and disciplined lives of our Methodist brothers and sisters in Southern Africa told us more by their deeds than their words was that for them Christ was truly Lord and that the primary preoccupation of their lives therefore was doing the will and word of their Lord unquestioningly and as a matter of first priority. What we discovered time and time again was that so far as the word, work, and worship of the Lord were concerned, they were ever willing and ready to make whatever sacrifices were necessary—and at times this meant great sacrifices in terms of their families and other personal interests—to faithfully fulfill their commitment to the Lord, and what is more, they did it with such joyful enthusiasm.

Needless to say, Christ and His agenda as Lord came first in their lives. To this clear, central command of the Lord, "Strive first for the Kingdom of God and his righteousness and all these things will be given to you as well," they obviously felt, and rightly so, that their one and only obligation as disciples was to respond in faithful obedience.

Impressive indeed was the inspiring joy and the passionate conviction with which they faithfully and obediently pursued the primary interests of the Kingdom of God—its evangelistic mission—in terms of its continuous growth and expansion by bringing more persons into the church and into the faith by any and all means, "in season and out of season." They were forever speaking about and sharing their faith, forever inviting friends, neighbors, and others to church, forever seeking as true and faithful disciples of Christ and servants of God to convert others to the Christian way of believing and living. They were thus engaged in the most effective form of evangelism, the type of evangelism that the first disciples, in particular Andrew and Philip (John 1:35–51); and the woman at the well (John 4) passionately employed with such spectacular success, the type of evangelism, which when enthusiastically embraced, is always amazingly productive; they were engaged, in a word, in personal evangelism and their boundless, zealous, and joyful enthusiasm about their faith guaranteed positive results.

In one of the churches we visited, a member shared with us how she and her family (husband and four teenage daughters) became active in the life of that church. A friend had invited her to the church numerous times, but she showed little or no interest until finally to end the ceaseless pestering from her friend, she decided to accept her friend's invitation to a special Advent worship celebration. The warmth, joy, love, and inspiration she experienced that first Sunday made her bring her entire family the next Sunday. They also enjoyed the experience immensely, with the result that in a matter of three or four months, they joined the church and have been active ever since. And she in turn through her personal passionate witness for Christ and His church has brought four other families into active membership of that church.

We heard many stories like this in the homes we stayed and in many of the other churches we visited of how God had blessed these churches with spectacular spiritual and numerical growth primarily because of the deep commitment to Christ as Lord on the part of the members and their enthusiastic zeal to contribute to the expansion of the Kingdom of God in their church through the passionate and persistent sharing of their faith in personal evangelism with others. Little wonder indeed that the Church in Africa as a whole is experiencing such phenomenal growth.

Tsitsi Moyo of Zimbabwe, Southern Africa, one of the first graduates of Africa University, a member of the Africa University choir that sang at 1996 General Conference (United Methodist Church) in Denver, Colorado, and one who also brought a thankful word of greeting to this General Conference from Africa University, is presently a graduate student at Boston University School of Theology and is planning on completion of her doctoral program to return to teach at Africa University. Prior to coming to Boston University in 1997, Tsitsi pastored the Glen Nora United Methodist

Church in Glen Nora, Zimbabwe. She reports that for the two years of her pastoral ministry at Glen Nora, church membership increased most significantly from 800 to 1200. And, as she shared, this marvelously impressive growth was realized because of the zealous and enthusiastic sharing of their faith with others by members that is a normal and natural way African Christians practice their faith as a matter of first priority in their lives and express their disciplined discipleship to Christ as Lord.

The recently elected Presiding Bishop of the Methodist Church of Southern Africa, Bishop Mvume Dandala, who is also a regional secretary of World Methodist Evangelism, at his consecration service at the athletic stadium in Soweto, challenged his two-million-member church to continue their fervent commitment to the evangelism dimension of the Church's primary mission: "We must evangelize without ceasing and let our teaching be transformative."

The vast majority of our Methodist brothers and sisters in Southern Africa live very simple lives materially but very substantial and powerful lives spiritually and what gives their spirituality its commendable power is the sacrificial nature of their Christian commitment. Their lives reflect and reveal a constant struggle to meet their material needs but also a dynamic faith that makes them "more than conquerors" through any and all circumstances.

Their sacrificial commitment to this primary mission of the church as determined by Christ is virtually a way of life for most of them in the way they live and practice their faith. Whatever the Bible requires, they strive to fulfill, even if it means, as it often does, sacrifice and suffering. Indeed, because sacrifice and suffering are such integral parts of their faith, as they practice and apply it, their Christianity may be correctly classified as a Christianity of the Cross. And therein lies its power, for a Christianity of the Cross is the only authentic Christianity there is. No wonder the church in Africa is experiencing such phenomenal growth, for a Christianity of the Cross that centers in and on Christ as Lord, as an absolute first priority in one's faith, in deed more than in word, has the transforming power to accomplish incredible experiences and expressions of spiritual growth both within the Christian and within the Church.

This contrasts sharply and significantly with the faith as practiced within United Methodism in this country. For the most part it seems that in the United Methodist Church, Christ is Lord in name only. Very often the Discipline not the Bible is the final word of authority.

In practice, it seems as if the Bible is primarily advisory and not always relevant to the crucial and current issues of the church. On the local level therefore, the administrative board or council exercises the right to determine what the priority agenda of the church should be in terms of its mission and ministry, sometimes in total disregard of the mission and mandate given by Christ. The local church functions in all respects more as a church within United Methodism than as the Church of Jesus Christ. Thus the church, for whatever reason, may not see the need or obligation to make the biblical mandate as given by Christ its absolute mandate—the evangelistic mandate that is—as a matter of first priority.

Christ therefore ends up having little or no authority in His own Church, the Church for which He sacrificed and gave His life. He is therefore for all intents and purposes Lord of that Church in name only and thus finds it necessary, to pose this relevant question to this Church: "Why call me Lord, Lord and do not do what I tell you" (Luke 6:46). And maybe He is Lord of the Church in name only because He is not fully Lord in the lives of the members. And He is not fully Lord in the lives of the members because in terms of their faith, they have not put first things first. For again the first order of business for the Christian as for the Church is the order given by Christ: "Seek first the Kingdom of God and his righteousness and all other things will be yours as well" (Matthew 6:33).

Further, the faith of American United Methodists for the most part seems to carry no passionate conviction, as it most obviously and admirably does with our Methodists brothers and sisters in Southern Africa. Consequently the type of personal evangelism shared with such zeal and enthusiasm that is so normal and natural among African Methodists and indeed African Christians in general and is attended with such spectacular results is almost nonexistent in United Methodist circles in this country. And even if personal evangelism were the rule here among United Methodists, the results would most certainly be far less impressive than in Southern Africa, for if in sharing our faith we appear not to be passionately convinced and joyfully committed to it, chances are we will not be very successful in convincing others.

Again, the element of sacrifice, which is such an integral ingredient in the faith of Methodists in Southern Africa, contrasts very clearly with the faith of United Methodists here.

Sacrifice is a word rarely mentioned let alone practiced among United Methodists. How far indeed have we drifted and departed from authentic Methodist discipline, particularly that of John Wesley himself, for whom sacrifice was not simply a vital part but a daily and practical expression of the discipline of one's faith—essentially what Wesley understood by the challenging conditions of Christian discipleship given by Christ: "If any want to become my followers, let them deny themselves and take up their cross daily and follow me" (Luke 9:23).

What seems to be the key ingredient in the practical expression and application of our faith as United Methodists is not sacrifice but comfort and convenience. In an affluent and very materialistic society, where the focus is so much on material comfort and convenience and never on sacrifice, we have allowed our culture instead of the Word of God to be the primary determinant and influence on the way we practice our faith. Unlike our Methodist brothers and sisters in Southern Africa, we do not feel an absolute obligation to obey the will and word of Christ as Lord, regardless of the sacrifice or cost it requires but feel a more important obligation to justify or rationalize why we cannot obey the Word of God and the rationalization usually is because of the culture and the times in which we live.

Thus if the true cost of Christian discipleship involves sacrifice, as it always does, we are prepared to go the way of sacrifice only if it is convenient for us and only if it does not cost too much in terms of our personal comfort and material well-being. But of course true sacrifice by its very nature is not and cannot be a matter of convenience, for if it is convenient for us, it is not genuine sacrifice. In reality therefore, our commitment as a matter of first priority as Christians is not doing the will and obeying the Word of Christ as Lord, fully and unconditionally, be the consequences what they may, but conforming to the standards of material comfort and convenience of our culture. We may say all the right things, and we often do, in terms of our faith and commitment to Christ, but our lives, in terms of the predominant influence of our culture on us, speak so much more powerfully and convincingly that our words cease to carry much conviction.

Thomas C. Reeves, a University of Wisconsin historian, writing in the magazine *First Things* and commenting on American Christianity as a whole, observes: "Authentic Christianity and the world are by definition at odds, but for most Americans Christianity has been watered down and rendered innocuous, like so much fast food. It has become easy, upbeat, convenient and compatible. It does not require self-sacrifice, discipline, humility, an otherworldly outlook, a zeal for souls, a fear as well as love of God. There is little guilt and no punishment and the pay-off in heaven is virtually certain."

In practical terms and somewhat in clear reflection of the primary values of our culture, we have amended Christ's absolute order of priorities for the Christian and the Church to read: "But strive first for the Kingdom of money and the power that it wields and all these things will be given to you as well," for generally it seems our first and consuming preoccupation in the local church is not the mission to the world mandated by Christ but the money we need to survive or to give us a new and or beautiful building or to increase our investments for a supposedly rainy day, a day that never comes.

Indeed what we fail to note and perhaps lack the spiritual depth to discern is that in many cases the reason why we may be struggling to survive financially, the real root cause of the problem may be precisely because we have not followed or fulfilled the biblical standard of first things first as already determined and decided by Christ but have substituted instead our own self-centered, parochial priority agenda, one that is preoccupied primarily, if not exclusively, with the monetary concerns of the individual local church and thereby misses completely the mission concern, which ought to be the primary concern of every church that acknowledges Christ as Lord.

Essentially therefore, Christianity as practiced for the most part within the United Methodist Church here is a Christianity of the culture in contrast to Christianity as practiced for the most part by our Methodist brothers and sisters in Southern Africa and by African Christians in general—a

Christianity of the Cross. In a Christianity of culture, the particular culture exercises the dominant influence in terms of the practical application of one's faith as a daily commitment. And in the culture of plenty in which we live, the materialistic drive for comfort and convenience rather than the spiritual drive for Christ and the Cross plays the more powerful and pivotal role in the faith we live and practice—a Christianity that places discipline and sacrifice, if it finds a place for them at all, at the fringe and not at the center of one's faith. Further, in our very individualistic and independent-minded culture, the Bible is not the final word of authority in terms of the Christianity we live and practice, but we claim the right as individual Christians and churches to decide and determine what parts of the Bible we will accept and what parts reject.

And in a similar vein, we may pay lip service to the cardinal Christian principle that Christ is Lord, but in actual fact He is Lord in name only, for as Christ Himself observes, it is pointless and meaningless, even bold and brazen hypocrisy, to call Him Lord and yet not do what He requires and demands of us in His role as Lord. We call Him Lord yet deliberately ignore His imperative word by persisting in doing what we want to do or only obeying His word if and when it is convenient to do so or if it does not impose too many exacting and sacrificial demands upon us. And in an affluent and self-indulgent culture such as ours, very often not mission but money is the matter of first priority in terms of ministry, both as individual Christians and as churches—not mission to and for others in the world and on a global level, but money for our own personal well-being and local interests as churches to contribute more towards our own comfort and complacency both as individual Christians and as churches. This constitutes and is expressive of nothing more or less than a Christianity of culture.

A Christianity of the Cross, on the other hand, as practiced by our fellow Methodists in Southern Africa, and generally it would seem by African Christians, is biblical Christianity. It is a Christianity that seriously regards and recognizes the Bible as the Word of God, the ultimate and final word of authority in the living of one's faith, and as such regards and recognizes Christ as Lord, in word and deed. The primary influence therefore in the practical application of the Christian faith is not the culture but Christ, not comfort but the Cross. Christ is the primary influence because in the recognition of Christ as Lord, both for the Christian and the Church, the first obligation necessarily is to obey unquestioningly, unconditionally, and unreservedly the will and the word of Christ as Lord. The servant or disciple does not have the right, the authority, or the power to change, amend or revise what is the clear will and word of the Lord.

And if Christ as Lord is the center and focus of one's faith in terms of influence, direction, and application, so necessarily is the cross, for one cannot fully and clearly understand the true nature of the mission, message, and meaning of the life and ministry of Christ apart from the cross. Thus the significance and relevance of Christ's categorical words in this regard: "Whoever does not carry the cross and follow me cannot be my disciple" (Luke 14:27).

What the pivotal role of the cross means in practical terms is that sacrifice is necessarily and inevitably an integral part of one's Christian commitment, so much so indeed that one cannot fully and faithfully fulfill and do the word of Christ as Lord without serious sacrifices. Authentic Christianity therefore is and means sacrificial Christianity. And a Christianity of the Cross cannot and does not set its own priority agenda because that agenda has already been set by Christ in His role as Lord, an agenda that calls upon both the Christian and the Church to embrace mission in and to the world as a matter of absolute first priority and to realize that such a mission cannot be accomplished successfully without some sacrifice.

In the practical exercise of one's faith, one does not pursue at any and all costs, comfort, convenience, and complacency to conform to the dictates of one's culture and one's own self-indulgence, but acknowledges the central and absolutely necessary role of the Cross in the mission and ministry of Christ and also the all-important words of Christ Himself. Christian discipleship is inconceivable if not impossible without taking up one's cross willingly, even joyfully, like our African brothers and sisters, embracing and enduring the necessary suffering and sacrifice that the cross imposes upon us, as we obediently seek to do the will and word of Christ our Lord. As Dietrich Bonhoeffer puts it, "Suffering and rejection are the summary expression of Jesus' cross." Death on the cross means to suffer and to die as someone rejected and expelled. Jesus must suffer and be rejected by virtue of divine necessity. Any attempt at thwarting the necessary is satanic, even or precisely where such attempts come from the circle of disciples, for it is intent upon not letting Christ be Christ. That it is Peter, the rock of the church, who incurs guilt here immediately after his own confession to Jesus Christ and after his appointment by Jesus, means that from its very inception, the church itself has taken offense at the suffering of Christ. It neither wants such a Lord nor does it, as the Church of Christ, want its Lord to force upon it the law of suffering. Peter's objection is his unwillingness to accept such suffering. With that, Satan has crept into the church. He wants to tear it away from the cross of its Lord.

This makes it necessary for Jesus to relate clearly and unequivocally to His own disciples the "must" of suffering. Just as Christ is Christ only in suffering and rejection, so also are they his disciples only in suffering and rejection, in being crucified along with Christ. Discipleship as commitment to the person of Jesus Christ places the disciple under the law of Christ, that is, under the cross."

Typical of the culture in which we live, and reflective of the human condition in general, we like to experience the joy of victory that Easter gives but try to avoid at all costs the suffering and sacrifice that are an integral, inseparable, and inevitable part of a cross experience. But authentic Christianity, a Christianity of the Cross that is, reminds us that we can never experience the true and full joy of Easter without going through the struggle, sacrifice, and suffering of Good Friday. A Christian joy that eludes the pain of the Cross is a cheap and hollow joy, a meaningless and powerless joy, a joy that is completely devoid of real spiritual triumph and victory, a joy in other words that is not authentic Easter Joy.

2

Transforming Mission Visits to Southern Africa

The Methodist Church of Southern Africa has experienced significant growth over the years to the point where today it boasts 2.2 million members. We have already noted the incredible growth not only of Methodism but of Christianity in general in various parts of Africa. Statistics by themselves, however, in any given field of inquiry or investigation never do tell the whole story. These statistics therefore, impressive as they are in and of themselves, do not and indeed cannot tell the whole story of Africa church growth, particularly and primarily since we are speaking about the spiritual realm of reality and life, a realm that by its very vital and vibrant nature cannot be fully, adequately or satisfactorily expressed within the rigid confines of cold, dry statistics, most revealing though they are.

It is thus the spiritual dimension and dynamic that need to be more fully explored and examined to get to the heart of the amazing story of church growth in Southern Africa. And it is this dimension that we will examine at greater length to get a clearer picture of the remarkable and continuous growth of Methodism in Southern Africa, in the light of our mission visits over the years to the Methodist Church of Southern Africa, and in and through this process or as a result of it gain some important and invaluable insights as to why

Methodism in this country, or more specifically, United Methodism has experienced such consistent numerical decline over the past three decades.

The Methodist Church of Southern Africa has been linked with our New England (United Methodist) Conference and before this conference came into being in 1992 with the former Southern New England Conference in a covenant partnership in mission for twelve years. The Southern New England Conference merged with the former Maine and New Hampshire Conferences to form the New England Conference in 1992.

The idea for this covenant was born with two principal purposes in mind. The first was to remind ourselves of the fundamental fact that as two church denominations, in particular two sister churches within the global Methodist family, though separated by culture and country, in terms of the one universal Church of Jesus Christ, we are to be sure partners in mission. Secondly because of the different cultural context in which both Methodist bodies have been called to do mission and ministry in the name and for the cause of Christ, and in the light of our common Methodist tradition, we have some distinctive and practical mission resources to share with each other that would be a mutual blessing to each conference and thus contribute importantly to the global mission of the universal Church as a whole.

In our covenant commitment with each other, a central point of emphasis is that we are not simply partners but are equal partners in this exciting and challenging mission venture to which God has called us.

The Pauline principle that as members of the local church we are all like equal parts of a body and that by virtue of this integral connection as we fulfill our unique and special roles in terms of our particular gifts, we contribute thereby to the efficient, effective, and productive mission and ministry of the church as a whole, is a principle not exclusively applicable to the local church but is equally relevant to the universal Church and the various parts of it in terms of its global mission. It is in this global church connection that these two Methodist bodies fulfill their assigned mission roles individually and in covenant.

> For by the grace given to me, I say to everyone among you not to think of yourself more highly than you ought to think but to think with sober judgment, each according to the measure of faith that God has assigned. For as in one body we have many members and not all the members have the same function, so we who are many are one body in Christ and individually we are members one of another (Romans 12:3–5).
>
> Now there are varieties of gifts but the same spirit and there are varieties of services but the same Lord and there are varieties of activities but it is the same God who activates all of them in everyone. To each is given the manifestation of the Spirit for the common good. To one is given through the Spirit the utterance of wisdom, and to another the utterance of knowledge according to the same Spirit, to another faith by the same Spirit, to another gifts of healing by the one Spirit, to another the working of miracles, to another prophecy, to another the discernment of spirits, to another various kinds of tongues, to another the interpretation of tongues. All these are activated by one and the same Spirit, who allots to each one individually just as the Spirit chooses.
>
> For just as the body is one and has many members, and all the members of the body, though many, are one body, so it is with Christ. For in the one Spirit, we were all baptized into one body—Jews or Greeks, slaves or free—and we were all made to drink of one Spirit (1 Corinthians 12:4–13).

Thus the covenant partnership between the Methodist Church of Southern Africa and the New England Conference

(UMC) is a covenant of mutual sharing of gifts and resources with each other to the enrichment of each other and to the enhancement of the global mission of the Church of Jesus Christ as a whole.

It is in this same mutual spirit of sharing between churches to the greater good of the one universal Church that Paul in the mission covenant between the church in Corinth and the church in Jerusalem emphasized the equal responsibility each church had to share with the other the gifts and resources they had each been blessed with: "But that as a matter of equality your abundance at the present time should supply their want, so that their abundance may supply your want, that there be equality" (2 Corinthians 8–14).

This covenant mission partnership between these two parts of world Methodism is expressed primarily in two ways. In the first place is the partnership on the local church level. Churches in our conference that have a strong mission focus and wish to channel that passion for mission in a global direction are encouraged to be partners in mission on an individual basis with sister churches in the Methodist Church of Southern Africa who share a similar interest. Currently there are fifteen churches in our conference that are in this covenant mission partnership with sister churches in the Methodist Church of Southern Africa. This sister partnership in mission usually begins with an introductory letter from the two pastors.

Churches are then encouraged to become closely acquainted with each other by sharing all about one's church, its mission and ministries, including also relevant information about one's community, culture and country through the exchange of letters, pictures or where possible fax or e-mail. As a result of this mutual sharing, a participating church from our conference, or its missions committee, may decide, as some have in fact done—though this is not a condition of the covenant—to help financially with a mission project of their sister church. Or the Sunday School of a participating church may decide, as again some have done, to have as their mission project for the year the sending of school supplies, toys, etc., to the children of their sister Sunday School, or to adopt a child from their sister Sunday School through monthly contributions, or again some Sunday School children or a particular Sunday School class may decide to have pen-pals from their sister Sunday School in Southern Africa.

Thus Sunday School children are introduced quite early and in a very practical and personal way to the global dimension of the Christian faith and the Christian family, as the family of God, and to the fact that as the universal family of God, it cuts across all cultural, racial, and national boundaries and, very importantly, they get to understand at the same time too that Christian mission is primarily global, not local.

In short the participating churches of our Conference and the sister churches in the Methodist Church of Southern Africa that they are in covenant commitment with are urged, within few broad guidelines, to explore the full potential of their mission partnership in whatever direction and in whatever ways are mutually beneficial and fulfilling to them.

The second significant aspect of this covenant mission partnership is the exchange of mission visits of both lay and clergy persons between these two sister denominations within the global Methodist family. These visits are of mission teams or individuals and are generally of a short-term, two-to-three week duration. Individual missions are usually longer. Mission teams are organized primarily with partnership churches in mind. Needless to say it is most advantageous and contributive to a stronger and closer sisterly bond between two covenant churches if members of one church are privileged to visit their partnership church.

Indeed what a most exciting and joyful realization of the ideal of such a covenant church relationship for members of both churches in this mission partnership to be privileged to meet each other for the first time! Methodist brothers and sisters from another culture and country, with whom you have been corresponding for some time—in some cases for a number of years—and perhaps also relating to on other levels of communication, you are finally and fortunately able to meet personally!

Then of course if the church has been contributing financially towards a mission project in the partnership church, a visit by church members would enable them to see the project first hand, and if the project is still in progress and the mission team is a work team, perhaps they would even have the joy, privilege, and opportunity of actually working on the project.

Also, the church itself or groups within the Church, e.g., Missions Committee, United Methodist Women, or Sunday School, that has had an important role in contributing towards the growing partnership with the sister church would definitely not miss this great opportunity to send with the mission team special gifts, picture albums, letters, etc., that would considerably cement and secure the sisterly covenant bond between the two churches. And of course when the visiting members of the mission team on their return report back to the church, the result inevitably would be a deeper sense of commitment to the partnership and a stronger sense of solidarity with their sister church.

The whole objective ultimately of this mutual mission covenant between these sister conferences of Methodist Churches, as already indicated, is that through the mutual sharing of the resources, each conference has been singularly blessed with both conferences would be significantly enhanced to more productively and effectively fulfill their one primary goal—mission—and thus make a greater contribution to, and in the best interests of, the Church of Jesus Christ as a whole.

The resources we have shared both as the New England Conference and as individual sister churches in this mutual covenant commitment with the Methodist Church of Southern Africa have been primarily financial in the number of mission projects we have funded over the years. We in turn have been blessed with the privilege of sharing in the abundant wealth of their great spiritual resources.

This mutual sharing of resources in this way has as its model and inspiration the covenant sharing of spiritual and material resources between the churches in Jerusalem, Macedonia, and Achaia as given by Paul in his letter to the church in Rome:

At present however I am going to Jerusalem in a ministry to the saints; for Macadonia and Achaia have been pleased to share their resources with the poor among the saints at Jerusalem. They were pleased to do this, and indeed they owe it to them; for if the Gentiles have come to share in their spiritual blessings, they ought also to be of service to them in material things (Romans 15:25–27).

As the new England United Methodist Conference, another aspect of our covenant mission partnership in global Methodism with our sister denomination in Southern Africa has been the exchange of mission visits, both individual and team missions, both short-term in terms of weeks and much longer. In the twelve (12) years of our covenant life together, a number of mission visits have gone from us and others have come to us from the Methodist Church of Southern Africa.

Mark Fowler and Jonathan Almond, pastors from our conference, made the first visit to South Africa, which initiated the covenant. In 1991 I led a mission team of ten persons, including Wilbur Zielke from the Northern Illinois

Conference and Rosemarie Bormann from the Methodist Church in Germany, who joined us in Namibia on a three-week visit there and to South Africa. Other members of the team from our Conference were: Don and Carolyn Gray, Ralph and Ruth Oduor, Carla Stewart, and Veta Daley.

In 1992 Richard Harding, a recently retired pastor from our Conference, with a genuine global vision of the Church in general and a burning passion for Africa mission in particular, went with his wife Shirley on a one-year mission to Maun, Botswana. Through their dedicated, committed, and very effective ministry, a new Methodist congregation was established in Maun. This church is now a part of the Methodist Church of Southern Africa, and like so many others in Southern Africa is experiencing exciting and enormous growth.

In 1993 June Tulikangas, a member of the Belmont UMC, Belmont, Massachusetts, went on an eighteen-month mission assignment to Namibia and South Africa. Her mission primarily was one of economic empowerment of church and other community groups through local self-help projects. June's mission at the Northfield Church and community in South Africa coincided in April 1994 with the political transformation, through truly democratic elections for all South Africans for a totally free, non-racial South Africa, with the final demolition and death of the diabolical system of apartheid. She played a pivotal role in both the church and community in organizing and educating the people in the democratic process of voting.

In the summer of 1995, another team went on a four-week mission trip to churches in the Methodist Church of Southern Africa. Partly due to increased interest of a number of churches in our Conference in our covenant mission partnership with Methodism in Southern Africa and partly through a curious excitement to witness at first hand the transformational changes in both church and society in a democratic and apartheid-free South Africa, the 1995 team was a twenty-five member group. This team was led by the South African pastor from our Conference, Edwin Jones, and his wife, Una. Edwin and Una, with their children Wesley (college student) and Michelle (high school student), were sent to us by the Methodist Church of Southern Africa as part of the covenant mission exchange program with our Conference. They came initially for one year, a period that was extended to enable Edwin to pursue further graduate theological education before turning to South Africa. Edwin subsequently transferred his membership to our Conference. Other persons, in addition to the Jones family who embarked on this "Mission Journey to the New South Africa," as the trip was appropriately called were: Donald and Carolyn Gray, who were also on the first mission trip and whose wholehearted dedication to the cause of Africa mission is most inspiring; Donald and Janice Hoyle, Ruth Young, Rebecca Stuart, June Carter, Rebecca Cunningham, Veta Daley, Tom and Barbara Ingrassia, Marge Magruder, Marjorie Stark, Robert Thompson, Stephanie and Susan Walsh, Don and Clarice Gothberg, Toni Panciera, and John and Janice Rhind.

Other persons from Southern Africa in addition to Edwin Jones and family who have visited us over the years as part of this mutual mission covenant partnership are: Bishop Printz, former Bishop of Namibia, former Presiding Bishop Stanley Mogoba, Mike Crommelin and Bishop Gill and in December 1997–January 1998 the Reign Bow Gospel Group led by Calvin Cornelson, whose dynamic and exuberantly joyful ministry in word and song brought to all who were privileged to hear them a dimension of inspiration and blessings that would long be remembered and forever treasured.

To briefly and accurately summarize the impact of our visits to Methodist churches and Christians to Southern Africa as part of our covenant mission and partnership with them, one would have to say first and foremost, and beyond question, that it was for most if not all of us a spiritual transformation. Whether we were part of a team or in individual mission, whether ours was a short-term mission in the sense of weeks or one of longer duration, the common consensus among all of us who were privileged to visit our Methodist brothers and sisters in Southern Africa was that we had indeed experienced a great spiritual awakening, one that will forever challenge us out of our middle-class United Methodist cultural complacency and spiritual lethargy.

What is certain is that as a result of our encounter and experience with authentic African Christianity in its Methodist expression, our faith in terms of its spiritual dimension and application will never again be the same. We were totally touched and transformed by the unique power of African spirituality, the effects of which, beyond any and all doubt, will always be and remain with us. Indeed it is the same spiritual transformation that Bishop Susan Hassinger and Dorothy McMahon of our (New England) Conference experienced on their recent visits to United Methodist churches in West Agnola that has resulted in our 1999 Covenant mission partnership with our sister United Methodist Conference in West Angola.

African Christianity, as we witnessed it in Southern Africa, is a deep spiritual commitment where Christ truly occupies center stage in one's life and in the church; where the primary pursuit, the matter of first priority, is indeed the important interests of the Kingdom of God on earth, the sharing, that is, of God's love in sacrificial, practical, and personal ways by whatever means, with one's relatives and friends, one's fellow workers and neighbors, one's community and one's country, the world that one interacts with by accident and design, from day to day and from time to time; where the Bible is passionately embraced, believed, and applied as the Word of God and the word of life; a spirituality vigorously nourished and sustained by the daily discipline of constant and continuous prayer; a Christianity whose distinctive and definitive identity is one of suffering, struggle, and sacrifice and in spite of this, or perhaps more accurately because of it, a faith that is joyfully and enthusiastically practiced and lived, one that is truly triumphant in any and all circumstances of life. In a word, African Christianity is a Christianity of the Cross.

To be sure it stands solidly and securely on the firm foundation of the Resurrection, but it is a recognition that one cannot experience Easter without first enduring Good Friday, that in the absence of a battle, there can be no victory, that one can only experience one's faith as the victorious, triumphant faith that it is when one has first endured the suffering, the struggle, and the sacrifice that are an integral, inseparable, and absolutely necessary part of authentic Christianity.

Little wonder indeed that Christianity currently is making such impressive, incredible numerical strides on the African continent, that its growth in Africa as a whole is nothing short of phenomenal, as we have already noted. What this growth clearly and convincingly demonstrates is the power of a Christianity of the Cross, for a Christianity of the Cross is in fact authentic Christianity, one that is always accompanied and attended with great practical results, spiritually, numerically, and otherwise, achieved and accomplished through the power of the Holy Spirit.

The Book of Acts provides positive proof of this. Peter, in his sermon explaining the miracle of Pentecost, emphasized that this new radical, revolutionary faith was fundamentally a Christianity of the Cross, for only in the light of this condition and context can one understand that it is primarily and triumphantly a resurrection faith. The spectacular result was that 3,000 persons joined the Church that day:

> You that are Israelites listen to what I have to say. Jesus of Nazareth, a man attested to you by God with deeds of power, wonders, and signs that God did through him among you, as you yourselves know—this man, handed over to you according to the definite plan and foreknowledge of God, you crucified and killed by the hands of those outside the law. But God raised him up having freed him from death because it was impossible for him to be held in its power.
>
> This Jesus God raised up and of that all of us are witnesses. Being therefore exalted at the right hand of God and having received from the Father the promise of The Holy Spirit, he has poured out this that you both see and hear.
>
> So those who welcomed his message were baptized and that day about three thousand persons were added. They devoted themselves to the apostles' teaching and fellowship, to the breaking of bread and the prayers (Acts 2:22–24, 32–33, 41–42).

Peter gave basically the same message to account for the miraculous healing of the physically handicapped man at the temple gate who was lame and unable to walk from birth. This time the sermon was attended with even more impressive results:

> But you rejected the Holy and Righteous one and asked to have a murderer given to you, and you killed the Author of Life, whom God raised from the dead. To this we are witnesses. And by faith in his name, his name itself has made this man strong, whom you see and know; and the faith that is through Jesus has given him this perfect health in the presence of all of you.
>
> But many of those who heard the word believed and they numbered about five thousand (Acts 3:14–16, 4:4).

This time however Peter not only preached about a Christianity of the Cross, but he and John actually experienced the cross to some degree, proving conclusively that if we uncompromisingly and unconditionally live the authentic Christian faith, in one form or another, in one sense or the other, we cannot escape the cross:

> While Peter and John were speaking to the people, the priests, the captain of the temple and the Sadducees came to them, much annoyed because they were teaching the people and proclaiming that in Jesus there is the resurrection of the dead. So they arrested them and put them in custody until the next day, for it was already evening.
>
> So they called them and ordered them not to speak or teach at all in the name of Jesus. But Peter and John answered them. "Whether it is right in God's sight to listen to you rather than to God, you must judge; for we cannot keep from speaking about what we have seen and heard" (Acts 4:1–3, 18:20).

Not only Peter and John but the other apostles also suffered a similar experience of the cross:

> When they had brought them, they had them stand before the Council. The high priest questioned them, saying, "We gave you strict orders not to teach in this name, yet here you have filled Jerusalem with your teaching and you are determined to bring this man's blood on us." But Peter and the apostles answered, "We must obey God rather than any human authority. The God of our ancestors raised up Jesus, whom you had killed by hanging him on a tree. God exalted him at his right hand as leader and Savior that he might give repentance to Israel and forgiveness of sins. And we are witnesses to these things and so is the Holy Spirit whom God has given to those who obey him" (Acts 5:27–32).

And when they had called in the apostles, they had them flogged. Then they ordered them not to speak in the name of Jesus, and let them go. As they left the Council, they rejoiced that they were considered worthy to suffer dishonor for the sake of the name. And every day in the temple and at home they did not cease to teach and proclaim Jesus as the Messiah (Acts 5:40–42).

When we proclaim the message of the Cross in word and deed, through personal sharing or in practical living, the Holy Spirit triumphantly gives the growth:

Meanwhile the Church, throughout Judea, Galilee and Samaria was left in peace to build up its strength and to live in the fear of the Lord. Encouraged by the Holy Spirit, it grew in numbers (Acts 9:31).

And of course for Paul, the preeminent apostle, apologist, and evangelist of the early church who proudly claimed that he was "crucified with Christ," an experience of the cross in a variety of different and challenging ways was the norm as "from Jerusalem and as far around as Illyricum I have fully proclaimed the good news of Christ" (Romans 15:19).

But whatever anyone dares to boast of—I am speaking as a fool—I also dare to boast of that. Are they Hebrews? So am I. Are they Israelites? So am I. Are they descendants of Abraham? So am I. Are they ministers of Christ? I am talking like a madman. I am a better one; with far greater labors, far more imprisonments, with countless floggings, and often near death. Five times I have received from the Jews the forty lashes minus one. Three times I was beaten with rods. Once I received a stoning. Three times I was shipwrecked; for a night and day I was adrift at sea; on frequent journeys, in danger from rivers, danger from bandits, danger from my own people, danger from Gentiles, danger in the city, danger in the wilderness, danger at sea, danger from false brothers and sisters; in toil and hardship, through many a sleepless night, hungry and thirsty, often without food, cold and naked. And besides other things I am under daily pressure because of my anxiety for all the churches (2 Corinthians 11:21–28).

Therefore to keep me from being too elated, a thorn was given me in the flesh, a messenger of Satan to torment me, to keep me from being too elated. Three times I appealed to the Lord about this, that it would leave me, but he said to me, "My grace is sufficient for you, for power is made perfect in weakness." So I boast all the more gladly of my weaknesses so that the power of Christ may dwell in me. Therefore I am content with weakness, insults, hardships, persecutions and calamities for the sake of Christ, for whenever I am weak then I am strong (2 Corinthians 12:7–10).

It was only as a result of the many ways in which he was "crucified with Christ" as a necessary and inevitable part of his evangelistic mission to win the world for Christ that Paul was able to experience and appreciate the transforming power of Christ that enabled him to triumph over any and all experiences of the cross: "Thanks be to God who leads us, wherever we are, on Christ's triumphant way and make our knowledge of him spread throughout the world like a lovely perfume" (2 Corinthians 2:14).

Following are some of the comments from our mission participants that eloquently express the profound and powerful impact the triumphant spirituality of our Southern Africa brothers and sisters, centered on a Christianity of the Cross, had on us:

"The faith of the people is forever strong."
"The way the people reached out to us in trust and love was very special."

"We have seen the power of faith in the face of oppression."

"I sensed a real love for the Lord and a joy that is sadly lacking in many of the churches here."

"I was very impressed by their mission projects and their willingness to share whatever resources they have. My feeling was missions were first."

"We were the ones being ministered to."

"This was the spiritual journey of my life."

"We saw and experienced things few Americans ever will."

"The people were so warm and generous! It was like being reunited with long-lost friends or family—and yet (in most cases), we were strangers. But we were sisters and brothers in Christ."

We sensed this exuberant spirituality from the very beginning of our visits. It expressed itself most memorably in the deeply affectionate warmth of their welcome. The great excitement and radiant joy written all over their faces and clearly obvious in their voices as they greeted us for the first time not only revealed a welcome that came genuinely from the heart, but one that was truly a priceless gift of Christian love that we will always remember and treasure. In fact the extremely warm welcome we received with such hearty hugs and loving embraces everywhere we went made us feel that we were really not strangers meeting each other for the first time but in fact friends, and even more than friends—family. We truly felt, in other words, that we were being welcomed by our brothers and sisters within the family of God, or as one of our mission members so accurately expressed it above: "It was like being reunited with long-lost friends or family—and yet (in most cases) we were strangers. But we were sisters and brothers in Christ."

As partners in ministry in this mutual covenant between our two Methodist bodies, the bond that united and knitted our hearts together in faith, in love, and in mission, and that was nurtured and nourished through letters, fax, and phone reached its highest point of fulfillment and realization in the enthusiastic joy of a personal meeting. This was particularly so, needless to say, for persons who were from churches that had a sister-church relationship with some of the churches on our itinerary. What an unforgettably joyful time of meeting and greeting! Such is the powerful spirit of oneness we celebrate as Christians in spite of all our differences, in terms of race, culture, and nationality. We understood then and in a much better, clearer, and more practical way what Paul meant when he spoke of the global Christian family united in Christ, which radically cuts across all human distinctions and differences: "There is no longer Jew or Greek, there is no longer slave nor free, there is no longer male and female for all of you are one in Christ Jesus." (Galatians 3:28).

And that oneness, which binds all Christians everywhere together in spiritual solidarity with one another, is truly transforming, all-inclusive, and all-embracing, as Paul further emphasizes: "There is one body and one spirit, just as you were called to the one hope of your calling, one Lord, one faith, one baptism, one God and Father of all, who is above all and through all and in all" (Ephesians 4:4–6). It was a bond we readily recognized and experienced in all areas and aspects of our mission visits to the Methodist Church of Southern Africa.

In terms particularly of the mission teams of 1991 and 1995, one of the primary blessings of these visits was the privilege, the joy, and inspiration of staying in the homes of church members in the various places we visited. They truly treated us like honored guests and made us feel very much a part of their family. This was convincingly and conclusively a consensus highlight of these trips. It was such a priceless experience, living and sharing in both material and spiritual terms with our Namibian and South African Methodist brothers and sisters and their families. Their generous, warm and heartfelt hospitality broke down all cultural, racial, and other barriers so quickly and so completely that it was just a short time before we felt as if we were indeed a part of their individual families. They went out of their way, sacrificially, to make us feel at home and were prepared to go to any lengths, if necessary, to cater to any special needs. Everything they did for us and gave us while we were in their homes was made all the more meaningful and memorable primarily because it was clearly touched by the genuineness of their love and care, a genuineness of caring and sharing that we felt and sensed throughout our stay.

An important part of their hospitality was the delicious food they prepared. Our experience led us to the conclusion that to be authentic, a southern African meal had to have three distinguishing and delightful marks of identity—great quality, great quantity, and great variety. Everywhere we went, whether in homes or in churches, we were always fed well with the best cuisine and in delicious varieties. The remarkable and revealing thing was that the economic circumstances of the family or the church made little or no difference in this regard. Indeed, strangely but truly, some of our best meals were eaten among the poorer families and churches. What this said most clearly to us was that those families and churches that seemed to have very little materially, in spiritual terms they gave of themselves sacrificially so that we could have the best they had to give in both physical food and spiritual food. And at the end of our stay, as a tangible token and expression of the special and affectionate relationship established between us, we were always given a gift as a way for us not only to remember them but also to continue this bond of love and friendship newly forged between us.

Hospitality in biblical terms is not simply an incidental or inessential privilege but rather a very primary and pivotal practice at the very heart and center of one's responsibilities and duties as a child of God.

In the Old Testament, particularly in the patriarchal period, due to the nomadic way of life of the people in that culture, hospitality was regarded as a sacred obligation, not an optional undertaking. As soon as Abraham saw his three visitors, even before he knew who they were and why they came, his immediate and instinctive reaction was to extend to them a most generous hospitality. According to the standards of our time and culture, we would first want to know who these strange visitors were and what was the purpose of their visit before deciding whether or not they were worthy of our hospitality.

No wonder Abraham is recognized as the biblical hero of great faith, for he did otherwise: "He looked up and saw three men standing near him. When he saw them, he ran from the tent entrance to meet them, and bowed down to the ground. He said, 'My Lord, if I find favor with you, do not pass by your servant. Let a little water be brought, and wash your feet and rest yourselves under the tree. Let me bring a little bread that you may refresh yourselves and after that you may pass on—since you have come to your servant' " (Genesis 18:1–5).

Then for us too, if these strangers did qualify for our hospitality, because they came unannounced, they would perhaps be given the bare minimum that reasonably fell within the bonds of civility and courtesy. Not Abraham. Unannounced or not, these visitors qualified for the best that he had available: "And Abraham hastened into the tent to Sarah and said, 'Make ready quickly three measures of choice flour, knead it and make cakes.' Abraham ran to the herd and took a calf, tender and good, and gave it to the servant who hastened to prepare it. Then he took curds and milk and the calf that he had prepared and set it before them; and he stood by them under the tree while they ate" (Genesis 18:6–8).

The flour for the cakes had to be "choice" flour, and the calf had to be "tender and good." Again such words as "hastened," "quickly," "ran," "hastened," indicate that for Abraham his guests had to be given top priority. Whatever were the family commitments at that particular point in time, they had to be sacrificed for the welfare and well-being of his guests.

Then Israel, as God's covenant people, is assigned the solemn and sacred obligation to always welcome the stranger and sojourner, for this is what truly identifies her as the chosen people of a covenant God, and moreover Israel must never forget where she came from and who she was before elevation to the uniquely privileged status as the one and only people of all the peoples of the earth to be chosen by God—she needs to remember that as a people they too "were sojourners in the land of Egypt," thus the obligation and order to always welcome and love the stranger and sojourner. And to reinforce the central role of this law in the life and mission of this chosen community, Israel is reminded of this imperative duty time and again throughout God's covenant instructions to her: "For the Lord your God is God of gods and Lord of lords, the great God, mighty and awesome, who is not partial and takes no bribe, who executes justice for the orphan and the widow, and who loves the strangers, providing them food and clothing. You shall also love the stranger, for you were strangers in the land of Egypt (Deuteronomy 10:17–19: also Exodus 22:21; Deuteronomy 5:14–15, 16:10–12, 23:7, 24:14–22, 26:5–11).

Loving the stranger in the context of this chosen nation does not simply mean giving him (her) a warm welcome and hospitality, but it also means in practical terms ensuring that the stranger shares in and benefits from equal justice while he resides within the community: He (sojourner) participates in the assembly (Deuteronomy 29:10–13; Joshua 8:30–35); he is entitled to the benefit of the tithe (Deuteronomy 14:28–29); he is to be judged the same way as an Israelite (1:16), he is entitled to equal justice (24:14); he is expected to keep the law and observe festivals along with the native Israelites, joining in the celebration of the Sabbath, the festival of deliverance in the D decalogue (5:14–15), the feast of weeks (16:10–12), Tabernacles (16:13–14), the offering of first fruits (26:11).

And of course at the heart of equal justice is the fundamental principle that one law applies both to the citizen and the stranger or sojourner: "As for the assembly, there shall be for both you and the resident alien a single statute, a perpetual statute throughout your generations; you and the alien shall be alike before the Lord. You and the alien who resides with you shall have the same law and the same ordinance" (Numbers 15:15–16).

In the New Testament, hospitality was absolutely crucial, critical, and central to the early growth and spread of Christianity throughout the Roman world. Paul as he crisscrossed the Roman Empire in his zealous and relentless missionary drive to establish new churches and in his ardently ambitious goal of winning the Roman world for Christ by preaching "Jesus Christ and Him crucified" was completely dependent on the hospitality of his brothers and sisters in Christ in the various places he visited. Their hospitality contributed significantly to the success of his mission journeys. In writing to Philemon urging him to take back Onesimus, not as a slave but now as a brother, Paul also makes this final request of Philemon: "One thing more—prepare a guest room for me, for I am hoping through your prayer to be restored to you" (Philemon 22).

The Philippians so excelled in the gift of hospitality that their generosity in providing for all of Paul's physical needs was not limited to when Paul was in Macedonia but continued even after he left Macedonia on his ambitious global mission:

> I rejoice in the Lord greatly that now at last you have revived your concern for me; indeed, you were concerned for me, but had no opportunity to show it. Not that I am referring to being in need; for I have learned to be content with whatever I have. I know what it is to have little, and I know what it is to have plenty. In any and all circumstances, I have learned the secret of being well-fed and of going hungry, of having plenty and of being in need. I can do all things through Him who strengthens me. In any case it was kind of you to share my distress.
>
> You Philippians indeed know that in the early days of the gospel, when I left Macedonia, no church shared with me in the matter of giving and receiving, except you alone. For even when I was in Thessalonica, you sent me help for my needs more than once. Not that I seek the gift, but I seek the profit that accumulates to your account. I have been paid in full and have more than enough; I am fully satisfied now that I have received from Epaphroditus the gifts you sent, a fragrant offering, a sacrifice acceptable and pleasing to God. And my God will fully satisfy every need of yours according to his riches in glory in Christ Jesus. To our God and father be glory forever and ever. Amen (Philippians 4:10–20).

To the church in Rome, Paul emphasizes the importance of "hospitality to strangers" in the whole mission of the Church, a point that is made with similar conviction by the author of Hebrews (Romans 12:13; Hebrews 13:2). Indeed one gets a clearer understanding of how vital hospitality was to the mission and ministry of the early Church in light of the fact that this was one of the primary qualifications required of a bishop. "For a bishop, as God's steward, must be blameless; he must not be arrogant or quick-tempered or addicted to wine or violent or greedy for gain; but he must be hospitable, a lover of goodness, prudent, upright, devout and self-controlled. He must have a firm grasp of the word that is trustworthy in accordance with the teaching so that he may be able both to preach with sound doctrine and to refute those who contradict it" (Titus 1:7–9; 1 Timothy 3:1–7).

And of course in the ministry of Jesus, hospitality assumed an indispensable role, primarily because of the homeless nature of His life, as He identified fully and completely with the poorest of the poor, the destitute, the deprived and the dispossessed, the homeless and the helpless, and those who were struggling, suffering, and subsisting, in a precarious existence, on the very margins of life and society. "And Jesus said to him, 'Foxes have holes and birds of the air have nests; but the Son of Man has nowhere to lay his head' " (Luke 9:58).

The gospels reveal several instances in which His followers ministered to Him through their hospitality, which necessarily and reasonably leads one to the conclusion that there were countless others too numerous to mention who catered to His physical needs for bed and board throughout the entire course of His ministry (Luke 7:36; 8:1–3; 9:51–53; 10:38–39; 14:1, 19:3–6; John 12:1–2).

Jesus further emphasized what an integral and vitally important function hospitality fulfilled in the early success and growth of Christianity in the mission charge that He gave to His disciples, as they embarked on their first evangelistic venture. Those places and people that refused to welcome them and denied them hospitality inevitably qualified for divine disfavor and judgment: "He said to them,

'The harvest is plentiful, but the laborers are few; therefore ask the Lord of the harvest to send out laborers into His harvest. Go on your way. See, I am sending you out like lambs into the midst of wolves. Carry no purse, no bag, no sandals; and greet no one on the road. Whatever house you enter, first say 'Peace to this house!' And if anyone is there who shares in peace, your peace will rest on that person, but if not, it will return to you. Remain in the same house eating and drinking whatever they provide, for the laborer deserves to be paid. Do not move from house to house. Whenever you enter a town and its people welcome you, eat what is set before you; cure the sick who are there, and say to them: 'The Kingdom of God has come near to you.' But whenever you enter a town and they do not welcome you, go out into the streets and say, 'Even the dust of your town that clings to our feet, we wipe off in protest against you. Yet know this: the Kingdom of God has come near.' I tell you, on that day it will be more tolerable for Sodom than for that town (Luke 10:1–12).

But for Jesus hospitality was not only a cardinal Christian virtue, invaluably instrumental to the growth of the faith, but even more, it is one of the indispensable conditions for entry into the eternal Kingdom. One can enter into the Kingdom of God only if one faithfully practices genuine Christian hospitality, among other necessary commitments to the poor and powerless:

Then the King will say to those at his right hand, 'Come, you that are blessed by my Father, inherit the Kingdom prepared for you from the foundation of the world; for I was hungry and you gave me food, I was thirsty and you gave me something to drink, I was a stranger and you welcomed me, I was naked and you gave me clothing, I was sick and you took care of me, I was in prison and you visited me.' Then the righteous will answer him, 'Lord, when was it that we saw you hungry and gave you food, or thirsty and gave you something to drink? And when was it that we saw you a stranger and welcomed you, or naked and gave you clothing? And when was it that we saw you sick or in prison and visited you?' And the King will answer them, 'Truly I tell you, just as you did it to one of the least of these who are members of my family you did it to me' (Matthew 25:34–40).

The Methodist Church of Southern Africa and indeed the Church in Southern Africa as a whole possess in impressive measure many spiritual gifts, but among the most prominent and potent to be sure is their gift of hospitality. Their joyful warmth and great generosity of spirit, coming as it does from the heart, makes you feel genuinely welcome to their churches and their homes. And what gives their hospitality its most powerful appeal, what makes it authentically Christian is its sacrificial quality. The vast majority of our Southern Africa brothers and sisters do not, needless to say, live a life of material abundance, but they give of themselves and what they have so sacrificially and so genuinely and share together and with each other so freely and so frequently that the little that they have does indeed become much. Their welcome whether at church or home always gives you the feeling of being special and the sense that you stand with them on common ground as brothers and sisters in Christ and that therefore you belong equally with them to their community of faith.

And theirs is indeed a natural, unforced hospitality, because it is another true and practical expression of their spirituality, a spirituality whose distinguishing characteristic is the principle of sacrifice, the principle that is at the heart of a Christianity of the Cross.

Sacrifice as a way of life in the practical application of the faith is a commitment enthusiastically embraced at all levels of ministry within the Methodist Church of Southern Africa. I personally experienced it not only in churches and in homes of individual church members and pastors, but also in the homes of bishops, including that of then-Presiding Bishop, Stanley and Mrs. Mogoba. I was also privileged to enjoy and experience the great and generous hospitality of the Bishop of Namibia, Bishop F. Prinz and his family and Bishop Mike Crockett and his family.

Bishop Prinz was primarily responsible for organizing the 1991 trip and did such a brilliant job in putting together the itinerary and making all the necessary arrangements that the trip was a marvelous blessing and success, in terms of its mission, one that we will always treasure and remember most fondly.

The commendable spirit of sacrifice so typical of African Christianity was not only an important part of the warm joyful and enthusiastic hospitality that I received at their homes but significantly, too, the time they gave to our mission. For the three weeks we were in Namibia, Bishop Prinz personally accompanied us at every point of our itinerary, needless to say at significant sacrifice to his regular and very demanding episcopal and administrative schedule. And for the few days I was in Sassolburg and Durban, even though at very short notice, Bishop Crockett and Presiding Bishop Mogoba personally took me to a number of places of mission, ministry, and cultural interests that were not on our itinerary. Such indeed is the impressive and convincing nature of sacrifice in Southern Africa Christianity and spirituality.

Thus Southern Africa Christian hospitality, as we experienced it, radiated with much joy, warmth, friendship, fellowship, sacrifice and love. It clearly, consistently and convincingly conveyed the message that as their guests we were not strangers and we were not simply friends—rather we were family, brothers and sisters in Christ. Therefore they shared their very best with us, in the true Christian spirit revealed in Hebrews 13:16:"Do not neglect to do good and to share what you have, for such sacrifices are pleasing to God."

But it was not just the material things that come with good hospitality that made the difference—more enduringly it was their giving of themselves to us so freely and generously in terms of time and interests, their gentle, joyful, loving spirit, their willingness to make sacrifices on our behalf and of course their hearty affectionate hugs—these are the important ingredients of their hospitality that told us more powerfully and persuasively than words ever could that we were truly welcome. Such quality hospitality, it goes without saying, immediately, spontaneously, and completely broke down any and all such dividing walls as culture, class, race, and nationality between us and made us sense that one common bond between us, that uniquely Christian feeling that despite all external differences, we are truly one in the spirit, one in the Lord.

Little wonder then that Methodism in Southern Africa and the Church in Southern Africa as a whole is experiencing such spectacular growth. The unforgettably warm welcome and hospitality that we who participated in mission visits to Southern Africa experienced, both groups and individuals, a genuine, heartfelt welcome and hospitality so typical of churches in Africa in general, speak most eloquently to an important reason for Africa church growth. Persons and families who visit these churches for the first time and are warmly welcomed by this type of friendly, genuine, and gracious hospitality, one that comes from the heart and expresses itself in deeds more than words, in a spirit of joyful sharing and caring, a hospitality that readily breaks down barriers between people and quickly gives one the feeling that one is among friends and family, not strangers—such persons and families will return to these churches not simply for a second visit but to be part of such a loving, caring extended church family, one whose family members are willing to make whatever sacrifices are necessary for the welfare and well-being of one another, having regard to the very strong, solid, and sacred family bond that thrives among Africans generally.

This contrasts sharply and strikingly with the welcome and hospitality as generally practiced in many of our churches in this country and explains in some measure the consistently declining numbers within our Church. And here again the cultural influence is so predominant and powerful that what takes place in the area of welcome and hospitality in the Church is precisely but perilously what the culture dictates and determines. In our very impersonal and self-centered culture, one that is inherently distrustful of all strangers, and where one is always so busy and preoccupied with matters of one's own personal concern that one has little or no time for or interest in the concerns and well-being of others, particularly if they are strangers, the welcome and hospitality we extend to visitors in our churches is for the most part not warm and friendly but cold and distant, at best perfunctory and routine, at worst discourteous or rude, consciously or unconsciously. And surprise of surprises, we wonder why they never come back.

In our narcissistic culture of comfort and convenience, where we fervently, even at times passionately, pursue personal comfort at all costs, we are generally either unwilling or unable to make whatever sacrifices of time or personal interests may be necessary to make the stranger or visitor really feel welcome and comfortable among us because it is not convenient for us to do so or perhaps because it does not fit in with our personal plans. In this regard Paul reminds us that true commitment to our faith imposes upon us the obligation to practice the Christian principle of sacrifice on behalf of others, not conform to the cultural standards of convenience and personal self-interest: "If then there is any encouragement in Christ, any consolation from love, any sharing in the spirit, any compassion and sympathy, make my joy complete; be of the same mind, having the same love, being in full accord and of one mind. Do nothing from selfish ambition or conceit, but in humility regard others as better than yourselves. Let each of you look not to your own interests but to the interests of others" (Philippians 2:1–4).

Also we may pay lip service to the fact that we are brothers and sisters to all Christians around the world, whomever they might be, within the unique and universal family of God, and that further we should regard and recognize all persons, regardless of culture, class, race, nationality, sexual orientation, or other difference, of equal worth and integrity as children of God, who should be treated as such, as Christian love requires and as Christian justice demands.

Consistently, however, our actions tell a different story. Quite often we are not very brotherly and sisterly in our welcome and hospitality to fellow Christians who may be visiting our churches for the first time in their search for a new faith community, with the result that they feel very much like strangers in our churches instead of brothers and sisters. Needless to say such persons would rarely if ever return for a second visit but would simply continue their search for a church where they would feel more welcome, where they would feel as if they are truly among brothers and sisters who genuinely care about them and each other in a loving, happy, close-knit church family, whose primary goal is the mission of Christ in the community and in the world.

Again in this area of welcome and hospitality, many times we are clearly guilty, consciously or unconsciously, of one of the gravest sins of the faith—having one standard of welcome and hospitality for some visitors and another standard for others, on the basis of either culture, class, race, gender, nationality or sexual orientation.

James in his epistle categorically condemns this flagrantly unchristian practice, for it certainly makes a tragic mockery of the fundamental principle of equality of all of God's children, a principle that is at the heart of our faith and that should be the guiding influence on how we relate in Christian love to all persons: "My brothers and sisters, do you with your acts of favoritism really believe in our glorious Lord Jesus Christ? For if a person with gold rings and in fine clothes comes into your assembly, and if a poor person in dirty clothes also comes in, and if you take notice of the one wearing the fine clothes and say, 'Have a seat here please,' while to the one who is poor, you say 'stand there' or 'sit at my feet,' have you not made distinctions among yourselves, and become judges with evil thoughts? Listen, my beloved brothers and sisters. Has not God chosen the poor in the world to be rich in faith and to be heirs of the Kingdom that he has promised to those who love him? But you have dishonored the poor. Is it not the rich who oppress you? Is it not they who drag you into court? Is it not they who blaspheme the excellent name that was invoked over you?" (James 2:1–7).

If our churches are to experience significant growth, we cannot, as the author of Hebrews rightly reminds us, neglect the area of welcome and hospitality—"Do not neglect to welcome strangers" (Hebrews 13:2). Neither can we regard it merely as a fringe Christian concern, only marginally connected to evangelism—we do so with unfortunate numerical and other consequences for United Methodism and the Christian cause as a whole. It was vitally important in the history of Israel, as reflected in the Old Testament, and God signified its importance by constantly reminding Israel, not of her option, but of her obligation to welcome the sojourner and the stranger, "for you were strangers in the land of Egypt" (Deuteronomy 10:19). Further, as we have also noted above, hospitality played a pivotal role in the life and ministry of Christ as His words in this regard reveal: "Foxes have holes and birds of the air have nests; but the Son of Man has nowhere to lay his head" (Luke 9:58). And, to be sure, it was no less instrumental and integral to the incredible success and phenomenal growth of Christianity throughout the Roman Empire in and through the global mission of the early church.

But we need to welcome our visitors and share our hospitality with them, not with the cold formality or impersonal routine so typical of our materialistic culture, but in the joyful spirit and practice of our African brothers and sisters; our hospitality, including our welcome, to all who visit our churches should be with an enthusiastic sincerity and a warm generosity of spirit that expresses and reveals a welcome that comes from the heart, one touched by genuine sacrificial Christian love so that from the very beginning our visitors would not feel as though they are among strangers but, rather among brothers and sisters within God's universal family who truly care about them and their spiritual welfare and well-being.

3

Deep Spirituality

The truly Christian welcome and hospitality we experienced and enjoyed during all our mission visits to the Methodist Church of Southern Africa were not just a great and good attempt to impress us on how well they treated their visitors but rather were reflective and expressive of the deep, dynamic spirituality that we were all profoundly touched by throughout all our visits, a spirituality that was fully Christ-centered, one that was solidly anchored in their sacrificial love for Christ and for their fellow men and women, in particular, their brothers and sisters in the faith and in the global Methodist family. The deeply spiritual nature of their faith and its Christ-centered focus can best be expressed in what is unquestionably the most eloquent, passionate and triumphant declaration in the Bible of the incredible, transforming and absolute power of Christian love:

> Who will separate us from the love of Christ? Will hardship or distress or persecution or famine or nakedness, or peril or sword? As it is written, for your sake we are being killed all day long; we are accounted as sheep to be slaughtered. No, in all these things we are more than conquerors through him who loved us. For I am convinced that neither death nor life, nor angels nor rulers, nor things present nor things to come, nor powers, nor height, nor depth, nor anything else in all creation, will be able to separate us from the love of God in Christ Jesus our Lord (Romans 8:31–39).

Their abundant and abiding love for Christ was clearly evident in other areas. It was the primary motivating influence in the secure bond of love that drew them so closely and affectionately to each other as members of one church, as brothers and sisters of one community of faith, particularly when they were working together on a church or community project or event. It was such an inspiring experience to see Christians joyfully, productively, and effectively working together in unity and love as they were in the soup kitchens, youth programs, worship and celebration events, suppers and other church and mission projects that actively engaged their commitment while we were there. "How very good and pleasant it is when kindred live together in unity" (Psalm 133:1). The fact that they worked so lovingly and harmoniously together in a spirit of joyful unity is positive and powerful proof of their deep love for Christ, for when our love for Christ is genuine and deep, the inevitable result is love, peace, and harmony with others, particularly our brothers and sisters in the faith.

Christ in this regard reminded us of the two great commandments and the integral and inseparable connection between them: "And one of them, a lawyer, asked him a question to test him: 'Teacher, which is the great commandment in the law?' And he said to him, 'You shall love the Lord your God with all your heart, and with all your soul and with all your mind. This is the great and first commandment. And a second is like it. You shall love your neighbor as yourself. On these two commandments depend all the law and the prophets' " (Mark 22:35–40). Then in His farewell message just prior to His crucifixion on the Cross, Jesus gave to His troubled and fearful disciples a new commandment: "A new commandment I give to you, that you love one another; even as I have loved you, that you also love one another. By this all men will know that you are my disciples, if you have love for one another" (John 13:34–35).

It is often said and rightly so that one cannot legislate morality, particularly the principal moral virtue in all of life, the virtue of love, simply because it is a pointless, fruitless, and futile exercise to try to do so. No law or any other compelling instrument in society, or any other context for that matter, can make a person love someone he or she hates. Indeed the only success compulsion is likely to have in this regard is to accomplish more convincingly the opposite result—to make the person in question hate the other even more, if for no other reason than simply to show that he or she cannot be forced against his or her will on this issue.

If this is so, then what is the point of the above biblical commandments to love, in particular the new commandment of Christ? Does the fact that the commandment comes direct from God make a difference? In other words, could God make me love someone against my will?

It needs to be acknowledged that what makes us as human beings unique in God's created universe is that we are all created with a free and independent will. This in essence is what it means to be created in the image of God. And in the exercise of that free will, we are independent even of God in the sense that not even God can make us love and obey Him if we choose not to. The uniquely crucial and critical image or likeness of God that we bear as human beings, the highest level of beings in God's universal creation, is one of absolute freedom and independence. The concept or understanding of an infinite God that we subscribe to as Christians necessarily implies that in the exercise of His absolute freedom and independence God is not and cannot be constrained by any external force or power since His is the ultimate power.

God is thus limited, if limitation indeed it can be called, only by the limitation He chooses to impose upon Himself. In a similar way, though obviously not to the same degree, the freedom and independence with which God has created us is the authentic freedom and independence to be fully, truly, genuinely human in the free exercise of our own independent wills. Needless to say we exercise this freedom in a finite sense. But our finiteness notwithstanding, this is the one area of our moral being in which, as God Himself has decreed and determined, we are independent of Him.

God has given to us this most precious and priceless gift of a free will, and what God has given God will not take away, even if as a result we disobey, reject, or refuse to acknowledge Him as God and Lord. We will of course, eventually, in one way or another, bear the tragic consequences of our wrong choice, as Adam and Eve so painfully discovered, but the right to choose, whether to follow the way of the Lord or some other way, is ours entirely and absolutely. The atheists, the agnostics, the animists and all who choose to believe in a god or gods other than the Christian God, in nature or whatever, are all exercising their sacred, moral, God-given, absolutely free will to believe, rightly or wrongly, as they determine to be in their best interests and not necessarily as God would have them believe.

Then again, what about the commandment to love God and neighbor and the new commandment of Christ to love one another? In spite of free will, there is a sense in which the concept of love as law is relevant in the Christian understanding of love.

The point of love as a commandment in the Christian context is to emphasize the absolute necessity of love in our relationship with God, with our brothers and sisters in Christ, and in a universal global sense, with all our brothers and sisters in the human family, whoever they might be and whatever may be their culture, class, race, nationality, or sexual orientation. Essentially the message here is that in our relationship with God and in all our human relationships, primarily those of our personal families and the family of God in terms of our brothers and sisters in Christ, love is not optional.

To realize and experience the transforming power, benefits, and blessings of these relationships love is absolutely indispensable. It is the primary link or bond that binds us inseparably with God, with Christ, with those in our immediate family circle, with our Christian brothers and sisters and with others in the most enduring, fulfilling, and inspiring relationships of our lives. And when we express our love unconditionally beyond the narrow, comfortable, and congenial confines of race, culture, class, or nationality to those in need, whoever they might be, and whatever may be the nature of their need, then we are truly being brotherly, sisterly, and neighborly to them as Christ Himself defined "neighbor," for in the global human family in the Christian sense, we are all equally brothers, sisters, and neighbors together and to each other. Christ very effectively emphasized this point in one of His more familiar parables—the Good Samaritan.

To the lawyer who asked clarification as to who his neighbor was, Jesus replied: "A man was going down from Jerusalem to Jericho and he fell among robbers who stripped him and beat him and departed, leaving him half-dead. Now by chance a priest was going down that road and when he saw him, he passed by on the other side. So likewise a Levite when he came to the place and saw him, passed by on the other side. But a Samaritan as he journeyed came to where he was; and when he saw him, he had compassion and went to him and bound up his wounds, pouring on oil and wine; then he set him on his own beast and brought him to an inn and took care of him. And the next day he took out two denarii and gave them to the innkeeper saying: 'Take care of him; and whatever more you spend, I will repay you when I come back.' Which of these three," Jesus asked, "do you think proved neighbor to the man who fell among robbers?"

He said: "The one who showed mercy on him." And Jesus said to him, "Go and do likewise" (Luke 10:29–37).

The parable of the Good Samaritan stands most impressively as the classic example of authentic Christian love in action because love that the good Samaritan exemplified was true, unconditional, sacrificial love, and he broke all the traditional customs, conditions, and conventions in sharing it. He was not only of a different culture, class, nationality, race and religion from this helpless and hapless victim of random, vicious violence, but in fact historically there was cultural, national, racial, and religious hostility between Jews and Samaritans, for as John in His Gospel reveals, "Jews, of course do not associate with Samaritans" (John 4:9).

Of the three persons therefore who journeyed on the road where this unfortunate traveler was found, the one that anyone would least expect to come to the victim's aid would be the Samaritan. The marvelous and miraculous fact that he was able to transcend the confining limitations of culture, nationality, race, and religion in responding to this desperate human need is an inspiring example of the transforming power of unconditional, sacrificial Christian love.

What stands out so commendably in the case of this good Samaritan is that in this tragic victim dying on the road from a most violent and brutal beating, he did not see just a stranger or enemy of a different culture, nationality, race or religion—what he really saw was a fellow human being, a brother within the whole human family, beaten almost to the point of death, and thus in dire, desperate, and immediate need of help. And his great and good heart of compassion and love told him that in the circumstances there was no other option open to him but the duty and obligation to respond to his neighbor's need. Such is the transforming power of Christian love. Only the invincible power or transforming Christian love can give one the capacity to love in this practical, exemplary way.

A further noteworthy point about the Good Samaritan—one that emphasizes yet another essential, distinguishing characteristic about transforming Christian love. Maybe the priest and Levite needed time to think or pray about it. Not the good Samaritan. His response was immediate. In a desperate, life-threatening situation of need, he did not need to give himself time to think about it, bring it before a committee, or even to pray about it. The solution was simple and clear—do something about it and do it now! And thus he did.

While some sit forever on the fence and others are seemingly caught on the horns of a difficult dilemma and yet others are engaged in needless discussion and debate as to what course of action to take in situations of urgent, desperate, and life-threatening need, transforming Christian love always demands and empowers us in these situations not just to act but to act immediately—because not only the well-being but the lives of many may be in jeopardy if we don't.

The second sense in which the concept of love as a commandment or law is relevant is in the area of responsibilities and obligations to others. There is no such thing as love—or at any rate, Christian love—without responsibilities and obligations. But Christian love, if it is truly Christian, does not need to have these responsibilities and obligations imposed upon it from without by some external authority. Christian love is a law unto itself in the sense that it imposes upon itself these necessary and compulsory obligations and responsibilities.

The fact that they are self-imposed does not make them any less mandatory. On the contrary because they are self-imposed, they may even be more compulsory, for Christian love to others is anchored in one's love for Christ, a love that always seeks and diligently pursues, practically and otherwise, the best interests of others. One does not have the option to decide or determine whether or not as a Christian one would fulfill the responsibilities and obligations, as one sees it, that come with Christian love. One only has the self-imposed duty to love others in practical deeds of Christian responsibility.

While to be sure Christian love in its general application does bear some common characteristics so that it can in fact be readily identified as Christian love, there is no one absolute standard of specific responsibilities and obligations in fulfillment of Christian love that universally applies to all Christians. We are all not only different and unique as individuals, but as Christians we are all at different stages and levels of Christian growth, and this in itself guarantees that we will all from time to time have different understandings of what these specific responsibilities and obligations of Christian love are or should be. And of course if they are self-imposed, they cannot at the same time be universal.

The one and only universal rule of Christian love is the Golden Rule: "Do to others as you would have them do to you" (Luke 6:31). How each Christian applies the general Golden Rule in specific terms of responsibilities and obligations to his or her situation is entirely up to him or her. The Christian does not have the option of deciding whether or not to apply the Golden Rule. Application of the Golden Rule is universally mandatory on Christians. The specifics of that application is necessarily individual and personal, determined primarily by the level or stage of one's Christian growth. Paul's general characteristics of Christian love, as given in the well-known love chapter (1 Corinthians 13) of the Bible may be regarded in some sense as an amplification and clarification of the Golden Rule in its application to Christian love:

Love is patient, love is kind, love is not envious or boastful or arrogant or rude. It does not insist on its own way; it is not irritable or resentful; it does not rejoice in wrong doing but rejoices in the truth. It bears all things, endures all things (1 Corinthians 13:4–7).

Authentic Christian love cannot and does not have responsibilities and obligations imposed externally because such external imposition suggests a relationship not of equals but of unequals—a relationship of unequal power and authority, where one person has or arrogates to himself or herself the power or right to impose these responsibilities and obligations and the other has the duty of carrying them out. Authentic Christian love can truly exist only between equals. True Christian love does not and cannot exist in a relationship of unequal power, for quite often such a relationship is one of fear, particularly when the person with the power consistently abuses that power and consequently makes the powerless person in the relationship respond in fear instead of love.

And as John reminds us in his epistle, fear and love do not and cannot coexist: "There is no fear in love but perfect love casts out fear, for fear has to do with punishment and whoever fears has not reached perfection in love" (1 John 4:18). Love and fear cannot live happily together—indeed, cannot live together, let alone happily—and are necessarily and naturally in constant conflict because love is based primarily on trust and fear always destroys or undermines trust.

Love thrives and flourishes and has the potential to realize its highest and greatest fulfillment in mutual trust, joy, peace, and happiness when the persons in the relationship, first and foremost, recognize each other as persons of equal worth, dignity, and integrity before God. Christian love begins and rightly so with equality of persons, the fundamental condition through which, within the family of God, Christians relate to each other on whatever level as brothers and sisters and also relate to all persons of whatever race, class, culture, nationality, or sexual orientation as persons of equal worth, dignity, and integrity within the one global human family.

The divine principle of equality of all persons as persons before God began at the very beginning with creation. God established equality of persons as a central and fundamental fact of His creation. It began with the equality of the first parents of the human family, Adam and Eve. They were both equal as persons before God: "So God created man in his own image, in the image of God he created him; male and female he created them. And God blessed them and God said to them: 'Be fruitful and multiply, and fill the earth and subdue it; and have dominion over the fish of the sea and over the birds of the air and over every living thing that moves upon the earth' " (Genesis 1:27–29).

In the perfection with which they were created, Adam and Eve were both indelibly and equally imprinted with the divine image on their being as persons. As they responded positively to the divine command: "Be fruitful and multiply and fill the earth," all subsequent generations of people throughout the world, within the whole human family, likewise bear, by virtue of our first parents, the same indelible imprint of God's divine image and thus share in the one common equality, dignity, and integrity as persons.

Adam and Eve were not only created equal but were also created perfect. Indeed God's whole creation in its original edenic state, all areas and aspects of it was, beyond question, a marvelous and magnificent demonstration of divine perfection, for an infinitely good and perfect God cannot, or in fact would not, create that which is imperfect. He would not be true to His perfect, divine nature if He did.

The perfection with which Adam and Eve, the crown of His Creation, were created was so special, sacred, and unique that God Himself acknowledged with divine pride, perfect satisfaction with His global handiwork after the creation of His masterpiece—man and woman. "And God saw everything that he had made and behold it was very good" (Genesis 1:31).

To maintain this world in the perfection and goodness with which it was created, God established His first moral covenant with humanity through Adam, in which God delegated the responsibility of taking good care of His created world to Adam, a covenant that included an important divine stipulation: "The Lord God took the man and put him in the garden of Eden to till it and keep it. And the Lord God commanded the man, saying 'You may freely eat of every tree of the garden; but of the tree of knowledge of good and evil you shall not eat, for in the day that you eat of it you shall die' " (Genesis 2:15–17).

Human perfection and the perfection in nature as a whole however did not last long. Human pride, which resulted in disobedience to God's will, brought sin into the world, and with sin has come imperfection and all the disastrous, deadly, and destructive forms and expressions of evil that have afflicted human society and our world ever since. Adam and Eve's sin, of breaking the covenant with God by disobedience to His word in eating the forbidden fruit, turned perfect human nature into imperfect sinful nature: "So when the woman saw that the tree was good for food and that it was a delight to the eyes and that the tree was to be desired to make one wise, she took of its fruit and ate; and she also gave some to her husband and he ate. Then the eyes of both were opened and they knew that they were naked; and they sewed fig leaves together and made themselves aprons" (Genesis 3:6–7).

This act of disobedience affected and afflicted not only the first human family but the whole human family, in that its moral consequences extended for all time to the whole race of humankind: "Therefore as sin came into the world through one man and death through sin, and so death spread to all men because all men sinned—sin indeed was in the world before the law was given, but sin is not counted where there is no law. Yet death reigned from Adam to Moses, even over those whose sins were not like the transgression of Adam, who was a type of the one who was to come" (Romans 5:12–14).

"For as by one man's disobedience many were made sinners, so by one man's obedience many will be made righteous" (Romans 5:19).

"For there is no distinction; since all have sinned and fall short of the glory of God, they are justified by his grace as gift through the redemption which is in Christ Jesus" (Romans 3:22–23).

By virtue of sin therefore, all people everywhere within the one global human family, regardless of culture, class, race, or nationality bear the inherent human trait of imperfection. But though sinful and imperfect and even though in consequence we "fall short of the glory of God" or His ideal for us, our human imperfection does not erase or eradicate the image of God in us, the most dominant and distinguishing aspect of who we are as persons or children of God and the divine image with which we were created.

God's most priceless gift to us is still, for all practical, moral, and spiritual purposes, alive and well within us. Tarnished and scarred by sin it certainly is, yet it is still vitally powerful and real within us, so much so in fact that because of it we are all persons of priceless worth and value to God. Christ Himself put the whole issue of the inherent value of a human person in clear practical perspective when He emphasized that all the material value of the entire world does not and cannot equal the sacred, priceless worth of the life of one human being: "What gain then is it for anyone to win the whole world and forfeit his life? And indeed what can anyone offer in exchange for his life?" (Mark 8:36–37).

The divine image is what qualifies each of us to be a person, one of God's most important attributes, and what alone gives us the potential for incredible good and the ability to rise to impressive heights of justice, peace, and love in spite of the natural tendency and inclination to sin. We will never be able to attain to perfection as the only Perfect Person who ever lived, Christ our Lord, did. Nevertheless, as imperfect persons, we must constantly and consistently strive to realize the highest moral potential for good we are practically capable of, given our human limitations.

Thus the relevance and significance of Christ's command: "Be perfect, therefore as your heavenly Father is perfect" (Matthew 5:4–8). But the power within us for good, unaided, would not take us very far along the road to realizing our best and highest potential, for our natural propensity to evil ensures that these two opposing forces within each of us, the good and the evil, each striving for mastery or dominance over the other, would always be in ceaseless conflict and that consequently in our efforts to realize our best potential for good, we will be critically hampered and hindered at every turn if we try to do it exclusively on our own. Paul enlightens us on this familiar moral civil conflict for the Christian in his letter to the Romans:

I do not understand my own actions. For I do not do what I want, but I do the very thing I hate. Now if I do what I do not want, I agree that the law is good. So then it is no longer I that do it but sin which dwells within me. For I know that nothing good dwells within me, that is in my flesh. I can will what is right but I cannot do it. For I do not do the good I want, but the evil I do not want is what I do. Now if I do what I do not want, it is no longer I that do it but sin which dwells within me.

So I find it to be a law that when I want to do right, evil lies close at hand. For I delight in the law of God in my inmost self, but I see in my members another law at war with the law of my mind and making me captive to the law of sin which dwells in my members. Wretched man that I am! Who will deliver me from this body of death? Thanks be to God through Jesus Christ our Lord! (Romans 7:15–25).

To liberate us from this crippling power of evil and to enable us to win convincingly this internal war within us so that we can rise confidently and consistently to the level of our best moral potential in terms of practical deeds of the highest good for justice, peace, and love, we need to draw on the inexhaustible resources that the Risen Christ has made available to us by virtue of His resurrection. Again, His triumphant declaration: "All authority in heaven and on earth has been given to me" (Matthew 28:18) is a reminder that this comprehensive, all-inclusive "all authority" or power has been given to or acquired by Him to be given to all who qualify on faith for it and that it necessarily includes the power we need to overcome evil with good. In this connection Christ in no uncertain terms reveals how powerless we are without Him in this crucial moral struggle and every other Christian or human endeavor: " . . . apart from me you can do nothing" (John 15:5). And Paul reminds us what an incredible difference Christ makes in all issues of life we confront: "I can do all things in him who strengthens me" (Philippians 4:13).

Evil, however, both within and without, will always be with us for this is an inevitable part of the human consequence of sin. The victory over evil therefore that we are able to achieve and realize through Christ in this internal civil war is not a once-for-all victory, for the moral struggle within against evil with which we as Christians are engaged is a continuous ongoing struggle throughout life, one which we experience daily and for which the limitless resources of Christ are ever available and necessary if we are to courageously and consistently live the victorious Christian life. The victorious Christian life is also the productive Christian life.

A victory of the good and the right in our inner moral struggle is never an end in itself. It leads necessarily and inevitably to the practical application of our faith in deeds of love, justice, and peace for the welfare and well-being of our fellow men and women. It is the primary motivation and inspiration to do the good and the right in the community and in the world—and it is what gives us the passion, the zeal, the commitment to be an instrument and agent of change in seeking to liberate those oppressive areas and structures in society that afflict undue and untold suffering on the poor and the powerless. It is the whole point of this moral challenge by Christ in the Sermon on the Mount: "Let your light shine before others, so that they may see your good works and give glory to your Father in heaven" (Matthew 5:16).

But the indispensable and inexhaustible spiritual and moral resources in Christ, though available to all Christians through the ministry of the Holy Spirit, and without which we cannot win our constant and continuous conflict within for the good and the right, are not automatically given. We have to claim them. Thus the relevance of these words of Christ: "Ask, and it will be given you; search and you will find; knock and the door will be opened for you. For everyone who asks receives and everyone who searches finds, and for everyone who knocks the door will be opened! Is there any one among you who if your child asks for bread will give a stone? Or if the child asks for fish will give a snake? If you then, who are evil, know how to give good gifts to your children, how much more will your Father in heaven give good things to those who ask him!" (Matthew 7:7–11).

Luke adds: "If you then who are evil know how to give good gifts to your children, how much more will the heavenly Father give the Holy Spirit to those who ask him!" (Luke 11:13). The Holy Spirit never comes to us without bringing these resources of power to do the good and the right. In fact that is His primary mission whenever He comes to us.

The message that Christ emphasizes here, clearly and beyond any doubt, is the vital and absolute necessity of prayer for the Christian who truly lives a victorious, productive and effective life of faith. It is only through prayer that we gain access to the infinite spiritual resources of Christ to ensure us victory in the moral war within, for as already noted, we receive these inner resources of spiritual power and faith only when we ask for them, and since we are constantly in need of them for an internal moral conflict that is continuous, prayer for the Christian must therefore be a daily, disciplined commitment. This is one of the more important reasons why a deeply committed prayer life is an indispensable asset to one's spiritual health and well-being.

Thus not only is it impossible to live a victorious, productive, Christian life without prayer—rather it is impossible to live a victorious, productive Christian life without constant, regular, dedicated prayer. And so Paul in his first letter to the Christians in Thessalonica urges: "See that none of you repay evil for evil, but always seek to do good to one another and to all. Rejoice always, pray without ceasing" (1 Thessalonians 5:15–17). Paul's point here is that to repay evil for evil means clearly that in the moral struggle within one's life between the forces of good and evil, good is losing the conflict to evil presumably because one is trying to fight this moral conflict on one's own and in one's unaided strength. The only guarantee that would ensure that good overcomes evil in their struggle and in their lives is for the Thessalonican Christians to "pray without ceasing." Such a moral victory of good, consistently achieved, would enable them to "rejoice always."

Because evil can be so subtle and sinister, one should never underestimate its power, for one does so only at one's own peril. One therefore needs to be ever and always vigilant, for failure to do so may be ruinous to one's moral and spiritual life. And to be responsibly vigilant in this regard as a Christian means to be continuously in the spirit and practice of prayer. Thus Jesus warned His disciples: "Stay awake and pray that you may not come into the time of trial; the spirit indeed is willing, but the flesh is weak." (Matthew 26:41)

In the Sermon on the Mount, Jesus further emphasized the necessity of prayer: "And when you pray don't rattle off long prayers like the pagans who think they will be heard because they use so many words" (Matthew 6:7). The point of emphasis here is "when," not "if" you pray, indicating that the disciples were expected to pray as a vital and necessary part of their Christian discipleship.

And in the Parable of the persistent widow, Jesus taught not only the necessity of prayer, but that in order to be effective, it must be done often: "Then Jesus told them a parable about their need to pray always and not to lose heart" (Luke 18:1). But far more powerful and persuasive than His teaching on prayer was His practice of prayer. The gospels tell us that Jesus was always in the habit of retreating to the mountain or a private secluded spot to pray (Matthew 14:23; 26:36; Mark 1:35; 6:46; 14:32; Luke 5:16; 6:12; 9:18; 9:28; 11:1). If Jesus found it necessary not only to pray but to pray frequently, needless to say, for us prayer should be a matter of absolute necessity and priority, a spiritual discipline, which we need to practice with regularity and consistency.

But prayer is not simply and only a means of overcoming

evil in our lives. More importantly it is an expression of a vital and vibrant personal relationship with God. When we are frequently, faithfully and fervently in touch with God through prayer, it clearly means not only that we have a deep, continuously growing personal relationship with Christ but also that He is the center of our lives. And this is what gives our spiritual lives the transforming power to consistently triumph over evil of every sort and to be an effective instrument for Christ of peace, justice, and love in the world. James in his Epistle reminds us of the power of prayer that truly comes from the heart: "The fervent prayer of a righteous person is very powerful" (James 5:16).

The spirituality of our Southern Africa brothers and sisters is a deep and dynamic spirituality because it is rooted and grounded in prayer. Prayer is indeed an accurate reflection of one's true relationship with God, and their focus on prayer collectively as the church and individually as Christians is a clear revelation of a close relationship with Christ as Lord. A dear sister in one of the churches that we visited said it best in explaining how much as a church and as Christians they value and depend on prayer. "We live by prayer," she proudly asserted, and then shared in song these words of her favorite hymn:

Have we trials and temptations? Is there trouble anywhere?
We should never be discouraged; take it to the Lord in prayer.
Can we find a friend so faithful, who will all our sorrows
    share?
Jesus knows our every weakness; take it to the Lord in prayer.

She further emphasized that indeed they pray always and for everything. Prayer, she said, has come to mean so much to them because of the many struggles in life—politically, personally, economically, and culturally—they have had to cope with, and so they have found it necessary to seek God's help all the time. They never get tired of praying because they have come to know and experience time and again how powerful and effective it is.

We were always so deeply touched by their prayer. They pray with such intensity and sincerity, such passion and conviction, such fervor and faith that if this says anything at all, it says beyond any doubt that their prayer comes from the very depths of their heart and soul. And they converse with their Lord with such easy facility and familiarity that it shows convincingly that the Person they are speaking with is Someone they know not just casually but closely and very well. In the churches, particularly among the lay leadership, there seemed always to be a readiness, even eagerness to pray, perhaps because it came so naturally to them by virtue of habitual practice and joyful regularity.

This is in marked contrast to prayer as practiced—or perhaps, more accurately, not practiced—in most of our churches here. Living as we do in a culture of plenty and prosperity, we, in practical terms, do not feel the same sense of absolute dependence on God as our African brothers and sisters. Further, the proudly individualistic, self-reliant, and self-sufficient nature of our culture, which is deeply ingrained in us, tends to discourage us from seeking God's help through prayer, except in extreme cases of need that seem to be completely and clearly beyond our control. And because of our very busy and demanding daily schedules, attending to all the various material and other personal interests that we deem important and necessary, there is little or no quality time to invest in seriously cultivating a close personal relationship with God through prayer, beyond and apart from the question of need, except perhaps, now and then, for a fleeting prayer on the run. Little wonder then when voluntary prayers are requested from our church members, including those in leadership roles, they seem to be somewhat uncomfortable and very reluctant to pray. The opportunity to pray is not embraced with much eagerness and joy as in the case of our African brothers and sisters. The reason may be quite simple and clear. They obviously cannot seize the opportunity, eagerly and joyfully, to talk to Someone whom they know just casually or as a distant acquaintance.

Then too our very practical and pragmatic-oriented culture does not regard prayer very highly or give it a prominent place in its system of values because prayer is considered a passive experience and only that which is active, practical, and real in material terms qualifies for the highest place in such a culture. Thus the primary reason why, generally speaking, prayer does not occupy center stage in our lives as Christians and a larger role in the corporate life of many if not most of our churches and why we do not commit ourselves to it with passionate enthusiasm as an indispensable part of our spiritual life and growth is the powerful influence of our culture, a culture that considers the spiritual, the contemplative, and the passive as virtues that are of little practical worth or value. And so instead of holding a central and integral place in one's spiritual life, prayer finds itself more often than not on the fringes or the margins of that life, for, in actual fact, we seem to include it as an option for us only when it is convenient to do so and only when our very tight schedule of commitments to what we regard as more important material and other concerns permits it a place.

Little wonder that our church meetings quite often are as divisive, acrimonious, and contentious, if not more so, as the meetings in our secular society and culture, leaving some persons angry, others bitter, and yet others frustrated, dissatisfied, and depressed. If through constant and consistent prayer Christ is truly the spiritual center of our lives and if as we gather for our meetings He is indeed, through prayer, the primary influence and Guide at these meetings, then the Christian ideal of consensus in decision-making is an achievable and attainable goal. Paul in writing to the Corinthians challenged them in this regard as follows: "Now I appeal to you, brothers and sisters, by the name of our Lord Jesus Christ that all of you be in agreement and that there be no divisions among you, but that you be united in the same mind and the same purpose" (1 Corinthians 1–10).

Thus, as Paul sees it, consensus should be the norm when Christians come together, whatever the purpose or reason that has brought them together, if they truly gather in and through the name of Christ. The fact however that we rarely achieve or realize consensus at our meetings but more often than not division and dissension is a clear indication that culture not Christ is the primary influence at our meetings and that Christ is certainly but unfortunately not the spiritual center of all meeting participants. Our meetings may be Christian in name but in reality are secular and cultural because they lack the authentic spiritual dimension, namely Christ, that can truly transform both the spirit of the meeting and the decisions of the meeting into triumphant Christian experiences for all concerned on the issues at hand.

This powerful, spirit-inspired influence of Christ toward unity and oneness with others is effectively at work in all Christians who have a vital, vibrant, growing relationship with their Lord, one that is continuously nurtured and nourished through fervent, faithful prayer. The destructive divisions and bitter arguments the Church in Corinth was experiencing were due, in Paul's sharp rebuke to them, to their disappointing lack of spiritual growth: "And so, brothers and sisters, I could not speak to you as spiritual people but rather as people of the flesh, as infants in Christ. I fed you with milk, not solid food, for you were not ready for solid food. Even now you are still not ready, for you are still of the flesh. For as long as there is jealousy and quarreling among you, are you not of the flesh and behaving according to human inclinations? For when one says, 'I belong to Paul,' and another, 'I belong to Apollos,' are you not merely human" (1 Corinthians 3:1–4).

And of course if prayer is not a priority in our spirituality as Christians, it is clear that Christ is not a priority, let alone the first priority in our lives, a fundamental requirement of our faith, for obviously He cannot be priority in our lives if we are not on good and regular speaking terms with Him. The inspiring thing about our Southern Africa brothers and sisters is that one is never in doubt as to whether or not Christ is first priority in their lives in fulfillment of what we have noted as Christ's primary condition for Christian discipleship: "But strive first for the kingdom of God and his righteousness and all these things will be given to you as well" (Matthew 6:33).

Theirs is not just a Sunday faith—theirs is a daily faith. They are forever talking about their faith and applying it to all situations of everyday life. The privilege of being guests in their homes enabled us to experience in a more personal and genuine way the depth of their spirituality. As they shared, freely and fully, in terms of their own personal lives, their families, their jobs, their village or township—their country and its promising future, racially, economically, and otherwise, Africa as a whole, and of course their church, it was always from the perspective of their faith, a faith that is rooted in the Bible and one that thus emboldened them to interpret and to accept all life situations in the light of the Word of God. Theirs is truly a biblical spirituality, and it is a biblical spirituality because these are Methodists who really know their Bible.

In fact they know their Bible so well that they can usually find a verse in explanation of almost any experience they encounter, and biblical phrases and references spiritually embellish their conversations from time to time. The fact that they are always talking and at times joyfully singing about their faith, about the fact that Christ has never failed them, and that it is God who constantly brings them through various difficult and oppressive situations of suffering and need proves if nothing else that Christ and spiritual matters of the faith are indeed first priority in their lives and that these are truly their first order of business as Christians who seek in practical terms the Kingdom of God and His righteousness.

By and large United Methodists in our country and culture seem to give the impression that ours is primarily if not exclusively a Sunday faith and a Sunday faith that is pretty much limited or confined to the one hour of corporate worship. It is very rare indeed that one would hear United Methodists speaking about or joyfully sharing their faith, about God's goodness to them, and about Christ as Lord of their lives during the week in the course of their daily affairs of life. Some would deem it highly inappropriate, others would be embarrassed to do it, and most would perhaps feel that in their very busy, hectic lives they just cannot find the time to engage in such well-meaning spiritual concerns—it is a luxury that they simply cannot afford.

And of course the Bible would not feature prominently in any general discussion or conversation for the simple yet inexcusable reason that most United Methodists do not know their Bible that well. And in this important regard, they, lamentably, are not good Methodists—at least not in the inspiring and illustrious biblical tradition of founder John Wesley, whose whole ministry was deeply rooted and grounded in the Bible, an important fact that was primarily responsible for the incredible success of his global ministry, as he himself expressed it in his famous and familiar mission goal: "The world is my parish."

What makes our Southern Africa brothers and sisters, in particular those from South Africa, embrace prayer with such ardent and passionate commitment and make it such an indispensable and integral part of their spiritual life and growth is that they have consistently experienced and witnessed the transforming, even miraculous power of effective prayer. They are absolutely convinced that it is the power of prayer, more than anything else—persistent, persevering, prevailing prayer—over the years, including the prayers of concerned Christians around the world, that completely demolished, dismantled, and destroyed the monstrous evil edifice of apartheid and gave miraculous birth to a new South Africa, one in which blacks, coloreds, and Indians are now triumphantly free at last!

Michael Cassidy, international team leader of African Enterprise, a Christian ministry to the cities of Africa, in emphasizing the role of prayer in accomplishing the spectacular miracle of a free South Africa, puts it this way: "Prayer of course played a huge part in what we have seen. As Tennyson said, 'More things are wrought by prayer than this world dreams of.' We have seen that happen in South Africa. Since April 1992 more than 1,000 groups of people have been involved in a round the clock 'Chain of Prayer.' And just before the election, nearly 30,000 people came together at the 'Jesus Peace Rally' to seek the Lord for our land."

Then the impressive and remarkable knowledge of the Bible of our fellow Methodists in Southern Africa reveals another central aspect of their spiritual life—Bible Study. Theirs is a biblical spirituality because they have made serious study and reading of the Bible an important and necessary part of their lives. It is part of their self-imposed discipline as disciples of Christ. Their faith is a Bible-centered faith because it is a Christ-centered faith. Their deep and abiding love for Christ has inspired in them a great love for the Bible.

A member in one of the churches we visited, in answer to my question of how she developed such a good knowledge of the Bible that she could quote it so readily, easily, and accurately, said that she loves the Bible so much that she takes it wherever she goes and reads it every opportunity she gets—on the bus, in the train, while waiting for the bus or the train, lunch breaks, etc. It is the one book she says she never gets tired of reading over and over again because even if it is a chapter she has read many times before, she always seems to get fresh and new insights every time she reads it.

Clearly therefore there is one primary reason why they know the Bible as well as they do—over the years both at home and in the church, they have consistently been diligent and disciplined students of this priceless Book and it has been given first priority in their lives as Christians for no other reason than that it is the inspired Word of God: "All scripture is inspired by God and is useful for teaching, for reproof, for correction and for training in righteousness so that everyone who belongs to God may be proficient, equipped for every good work" (2 Timothy 3:16–17). "First of all you must understand this that no prophecy of scripture is a matter of one's own interpretation, because no prophecy ever came by human will, but men and women moved by the Holy Spirit spoke from God" (2 Peter 1:20–21).

And as the authentic Word of God, they have experienced its awesome transformational power in their lives: "Indeed the Word of God is living and active, sharper than any two-edged sword, piercing until it divides soul from spirit, joints from marrow; it is able to judge the thoughts and intentions of the heart" (Hebrews 4:12).

Then of course since Christ is in fact their Lord, their first order of business as His disciples and servants, as we have noted, is to do the will and word of the Lord. And they can only do the word of the Lord if they know what the word of the Lord is as revealed and given in the Bible: "Why do you call Me, Lord, Lord, and do not do what I tell you?" (Luke 6:46)

One thus gets the impression that for them, and rightly so, reading and studying the Bible is not simply an end in itself but rather a necessary means to the all-important end of being a faithful, obedient, and responsible disciple of Christ. One must not only study the Word, but even more importantly, one must apply the Word, for therein lies the crucial and critical test of true Christian discipleship. Moreover, it is only through study and application of the Word that one experiences authentic spiritual growth, for the Word of God is the vital and indispensable source of spiritual sustenance for the Christian. One cannot therefore grow spiritually, productively, and fruitfully without the Word of God: "For though by this time you ought to be teachers, you need someone to teach you again the basic elements of the oracles of God. You need milk, not solid food; for everyone who lives on milk, being still an infant, is unskilled in the Word of righteousness. But solid food is for the mature, for those whose faculties have been rained by practice to distinguish good from evil" (Hebrews 5:12–14).

"And so, brothers and sisters, I could not speak to you as spiritual people, but rather as people of the flesh, as infants in Christ. I fed you with milk, not solid food, for you were not ready for solid food. Even now you are still not ready, for you are still of the flesh. For as long as there is jealousy and quarreling among you, are you not of the flesh, and behaving according to human inclinations?" (1 Corinthians 3:1–3).

"Therefore rid yourselves of all sordidness and rank growth of wickedness and welcome with meekness the implanted word that has the power to save your souls. But be doers of the word and not merely hearers who deceive themselves" (James 1:21–22). "For it is impossible to restore again to repentance those who have once been enlightened, and have tasted the heavenly gift and have shared in the Holy Spirit and have tasted the goodness of the Word of God and the powers of the age to come, and then have fallen away, since on their own they are crucifying again the Son of God and are holding him up to contempt" (Hebrews 6:4–6). "I have treasured the words of His mouth more than my daily bread" (Job 23:12).

Reading and studying the Bible therefore both at home and the church seems to be a commitment at the very heart and center of their lives as Christians. Little wonder therefore that theirs is such a dynamic, powerful, and exuberant spirituality that touches others so profoundly. It is clear, convincing evidence of significant spiritual growth and vitality as church members, particularly those in leadership positions. Quite revealing too is the fact that Bible study is one of the more well-attended church meetings. Perhaps it is a recognition that one cannot fulfill one's roles and responsibilities within the church at one's most effective best if one neglects one's spiritual growth.

What is worthy of note is how very active and deeply involved the church leaders are in Bible study and prayer meetings. In fact some Bible study groups are taught and prayer meetings led by persons in various positions of leadership. The important message this conveys—and a highly commendable one indeed—is that church leaders are chosen primarily because of their spiritual commitment to their own growth as Christians and thus the spiritual growth of the church, whatever may be their other qualifications for the positions they hold.

This is quite a contrast, generally speaking, in terms of many of the persons who have leadership roles in most of our United Methodist churches. In many churches availability, not spirituality, seems to be the primary qualification to chair any of the committees and boards of the church. In fact very often if there are Bible study and prayer groups within the church, some church leaders are conspicuously absent from these meetings, thus revealing little interest in their own spiritual growth and necessarily therefore, less or no interest in the spiritual well-being of the church. Indeed it is not uncommon to have church leaders who rarely attend the Sunday worship service.

This lamentably is a reflection of the sad, spiritual state of the United Methodist Church. Needless to say spirituality exerts and exercises such a powerful and profound influence on the church as a whole, that, when the spiritual life of the church is in poor health, it inevitably has a negative impact on all aspects of church life. Most importantly in this regard, spiritual growth not only precedes but is a necessary prerequisite and precondition for numerical growth. Paul reminded the Corinthian Church that ultimately it is God who determined church growth: "What then is Apollos? What is Paul? Servants through whom you came to believe, as the Lord assigned to each. I planted, Apollos watered, but God gave the growth. So neither the one who plants nor the one who waters is anything but only God who gives the growth" (1 Corinthians 3:5–7).

Since it is God who gives the growth, He would only do so when the necessary conditions for such growth have been fulfilled. An important part of the planting and watering that Paul and Apollos did was to enable the church, through their ministry, "to grow in the grace and knowledge of our Lord and Savior Jesus Christ" (2 Peter 3:18). And to grow spiritually in the grace and knowledge of Christ is also to grow in the many ways of putting that knowledge into practice, that is, of doing the will and word of the Lord.

Local church leaders for the most part seem to be more vitally interested in knowing the Discipline (UMC) than in knowing the Bible, and more obsessed with applying the power that the Discipline gives them than in acquiring the power that only Christ can give, the transforming power within that would enable them to be truly exemplary Christians and effective spiritual leaders for the good of the church and for the glory of God. This is important in terms of the growth and well-being of the church as a whole, for if the leaders do not lead spiritually—their primary task as church leaders—the members cannot and will not follow, with the result that the church inevitably finds itself spiritually and morally adrift on a sea of material and cultural inessentials with no clear sense of vision or mission for the future.

And again Christ's all-important stipulation: "But seek first the Kingdom of God and His righteousness and all these things will be given you besides," is of relevant significance to the church as well, for indeed if we put the spiritual interests of the church first in terms of the Kingdom of God and His righteousness, then to be sure "all these things," including of course numerical growth, would necessarily and inevitably follow.

Southern African spirituality, somewhat typical of the spirituality and Christianity of Africa as a whole, is a triumphant spirituality and therefore an incredibly jubilant and joyful spirituality. What is most memorable and inspiring about the faith of our Methodist brothers and sisters in Southern Africa is that it is a marvelous and magnificent expression of real Christian joy. Whatever they do, whatever trials they face, whatever challenges they encounter, whatever sacrifices they make, whatever deprivation they experience, whatever cross they bear, whatever blessings they receive, whatever victories they win, in good times and in bad times, in any and all circumstances, they always seem to radiate triumphant Christian joy. If there is one exhortation of Paul that they embrace most heartily and identify with most enthusiastically, it is this ardent appeal of Paul to the Philippian Church: "Rejoice in the Lord always; again I will say, Rejoice!" (Philippians 4:4).

In spite of the fact that life for the most part has been such a painful and bitter struggle for the vast majority of them, that they live under such poor and oppressive conditions, and that they have suffered so much for so long, yet the remarkable thing is that they can still be so incredibly joyful. The strange paradox is that they have so little in material things and yet so much in Christian joy while we as American Christians have so much in material things and yet so little in Christian joy. The secret seems to be in their deep Christ-centered spirituality. And the joy that results from a Christ-centered spirituality is not simply joy, but a real, triumphant joy. It has its roots in an invincible faith, a faith that firmly and unquestioningly believes that in and through Christ one has the capability and power within to overcome and triumph over at all times any and all circumstances and conditions of life, however difficult, tragic, or oppressive they may be.

And this unwavering conviction, this absolute certainty of victory in Christ, however insurmountable the prevailing conditions seem to be, enables one to be always triumphantly and genuinely joyful. The battle may be long, but in Christ, victory is always guaranteed: "Who will separate us from the love of Christ? Will hardship or distress, or persecution or famine or nakedness or peril or sword? No: In all these things we are more than conquerors through Him who loved us. For I am convinced that neither death nor life, nor angels nor rulers nor things present nor things to come, nor powers, nor height nor depth nor anything else in all creation will be able to separate us from the love of God in Christ Jesus our Lord" (Romans 8:35–39).

And John in his Epistle also points to the source of true spiritual victory for the Christian: "For whatever is born of God conquers the world—and this is the victory that conquers the world, 'faith' " (1 John 5:4). And it is the certainty, indeed the absolute guarantee, of spiritual victory over the struggles of daily life and living that enables them to experience and express such an inspiring quality of Christian joy, that as Peter reveals in his Epistle, it is completely beyond what words can adequately describe: "Although you have not seen him, you love him; and even though you do not see him now, you believe in him and rejoice with an indescribable and glorious joy" (1 Peter 1:8).

On the other hand, the absence of this enthusiastic spirit of Christian joy in most of our United Methodist churches reflects, among other things, the inherent poverty of material wealth, relatively speaking, and its inability to satisfy, in any substantive and genuine way, our deep inner quest for spiritual fulfillment and happiness. To be sure it is more a hindrance than a help in this regard—no wonder Jesus found it necessary to issue this warning about the spiritual danger of wealth: "Then, Jesus looked around and said to his disciples, 'How hard it will be for those who have wealth to enter the Kingdom of God. It is easier for a camel to go through the eye of a needle than for someone who is rich to enter the Kingdom of God' " (Mark 10:23–25).

Wealth, including the material comfort and power that it brings, not only prevents one from entering the Kingdom of God, but it can also prevent those who are within the Kingdom from realizing their highest potential as disciples of Christ and as instruments of God's peace, justice, and love to the world, in particular the world of the less privileged, the dispossessed, and the oppressed. Our culture of material-ism has conditioned us to believe that material comfort and well-being is the only road to true happiness. And so we faithfully travel this road, only to find that the destination was really not the one we were seeking, for instead of inner security, there is fearful insecurity; instead of complete ful-fillment, there is total disappointment.

When as Christians we conform to culture instead of Christ and pursue material comfort instead of spiritual growth, we regrettably become ineffective witnesses for Christ and the Christian cause in the world. Comfortable Christianity is, to all intents and purposes, joyless Christian-ity, for the focus almost always is more on the comfort than on the Christianity and since the clear message of a culture of materialism is that money is the one answer to all of life's problems, the danger in this type of Christianity is that one is likely to seek a material solution to a spiritual problem, a futile exercise that always ends in frustration rather than joy. It is precisely for this reason that Christ further warned in clear, categorical terms: "No one can serve two masters; for either he will hate the first and love the second, or he will be devoted to the first and despise the second. You cannot serve God and money" (Mark 6:24).

Comfortable Christianity is also for the most part joyless Christianity because it seeks to avoid at all costs the experi-ence of sacrifice, and sacrifice, particularly on behalf of oth-ers, is an integral part of the whole experience of authentic Christian joy, for sacrifice is symbolic of the Cross, which is at the heart and center of the Christian faith as a whole. Comfortable Christianity seeks to avoid sacrifice because in our materialistic culture sacrifice contributes nothing to ma-terial comfort. On the contrary it completely undermines and ruins it. Therefore comfortable Christianity would have noth-ing to do with sacrifice because it spells death to the comfort that one prizes and treasures so highly as one's primary pursuit in life. It is also the reason why comfortable Christianity can rarely find a firm place in its schedule or priority list of commitments for prayer and Bible study, for these mandatory spiritual disciplines for the faithful Christian would necessarily imply a sacrifice of some commitment(s) that culture considered important in terms of what constitutes one's comfortable life and such sacrifice is therefore deemed too costly.

To be sure the most exuberant expression of Christian joy from our Southern Africa brothers and sisters that we were privileged to experience and that left a most lasting impression on us, one that we will forever fondly cherish and happily treasure, was their worship services. Worship for them is most enthusiastically synonymous with joy. Thus to worship God is in essence to be continuously in a spirit of joyful celebration. In African terms therefore, there can be no worship where there is no joy, for worship that is not joyful does not truly qualify as Christian worship. In this regard they certainly identify most heartily and passionately with the biblical understanding of worship, one that speaks of the worship of our eternal Creator, the Lord, not simply in joyful terms but rather in tumultuous and rapturous joyful terms:

Sing aloud to God our Strength,
Shout for joy to the God of Jacob;
Raise a song, sound the tambourine,
The sweet lyre with the harp.
Blow the trumpet at the new moon,
At the full moon on our festal day (Psalm 81:1–4).

Make a joyful noise to the Lord all the earth;
Break forth into joyous song and sing praises,

Sing praises to the Lord with the lyre,
With the lyre and sound of melody,
With the trumpets and the sound of the horn,
Make a joyful noise before the King, the Lord (Psalm 98:4–6).

Make a joyful noise to the Lord all the earth,
Worship the Lord with gladness;
Come into his presence with singing (Psalm 100:1–2).

Praise the Lord. Sing to the Lord a new song,
His praise in the assembly of the faithful.
Let Israel be glad in its Maker;
Let the children of Zion rejoice in their King,
Let them praise his name with dancing,
Making melody to him with tambourine and lyre (Psalm 149:1–3).

Christian worship, African style, is an unforgettable, heart-warming, spiritual experience. It is truly a most triumphant celebration of Christian love and joy. The excited, exuberant happy faces within the congregation convey and communicate a love that is deeply touching, one that speaks eloquently and powerfully of the close bond that ties the worshipers tightly together as brothers and sisters within a caring, loving joyful fellowship. And what makes the whole experience so wonderfully uplifting and inspiring is that one senses from the very beginning the marvelous and matchless presence and power of the Holy Spirit, so much so in fact that our hearts if not our lips say and sing these precious words with great conviction: "There's a sweet, sweet Spirit in this place, and I know that it's the Spirit of the Lord; there are sweet expressions on each face and I know they feel the presence of the Lord."

Paul exulted: "Now the Lord is the Spirit and where the Spirit of the Lord is there is freedom!" (2 Corinthians 3:17).

And it was this liberating and unifying power of the Spirit, so dominant and dynamic in our African worship experiences, that gave us all that "one in the Spirit, one in the Lord" feeling in such rapturous joy and celebration and at the same time set us so completely free from the bondage of time that we were often in worship for over two hours and didn't realize it: with such hearty, enthusiastic singing, with such delightful rhythmic instrumental music, with such thunderous clapping, with such swaying and dancing, with such vigorous shouts of praise and adoration and with such spontaneous sharing and such passionate preaching, these altogether truly contributed to us making a really joyful noise to the Lord and needless to say are experiences of worship that are permanently etched and treasured in our memories.

It is worship of this inspiring nature that also has a very effective evangelistic dimension to it, for once visitors come for the first time and experience this heartwarming, uplifting, spirit-filled joy and celebration, in such a loving, friendly family atmosphere of Christians, to be sure, they will come back again, and not only that, but they would also share the good news with their friends.

In contrast, the powerful cultural influence of our society has so thoroughly permeated all areas and aspects of American life, even corporate Christian worship in our churches, that most often it seems, our Sunday worship services are anything but joyful. The true spirit of genuine Christian celebration seems generally to be noticeably absent from our Sunday worship experiences.

Somewhat typical of the form that middle class America—particularly suburban, middle-class America—is most familiar and comfortable with, the business model, the predominantly suburban middle class United Methodist Church, for most part, structures its worship service as if it were a business meeting, with the various parts of the service listed in the bulletin as the items on the agenda of the meeting. So slavish it would seem is the commitment to the bulletin that as it is inconceivable to have a business meeting without a printed agenda, so it is somewhat inconceivable to have a worship service without a printed bulletin.

Our approach to Christian worship is too seriously businesslike. Persons attend the worship service not with joyful expression as if truly rejoicing and sharing in a marvelously and delightfully spiritual experience with each other in praise and celebration of Christ our Lord, but rather they attend the worship service with joyless expressions on their faces as if attending just another business or other secular meeting.

Further, one needs to follow rather rigidly and legalistically—as in an agenda—the order of service as printed, with little or no variation—what is not listed in the bulletin should not be included in the service. The unspoken rule seems to be: there shall be no surprises in the worship service. Everything must be in proper order, and every item must be in its rightful and regular place and must conform fully to the general expectation. And of course, most importantly, and to be sure, reflective of our very time-obsessed and time-driven culture and society, formal worship must be strictly limited to one hour and on no account should it go beyond this absolute and arbitrary set time of convenience, regardless of whether real worship has actually been experienced, so as not to contribute to the discomfort or even incur the wrath of worshipers.

Small wonder then that there seems to be so little or virtually no joy in our worship services but so much joy in the worship services of our sister churches in Africa. The radical difference is the Spirit of God. On the one hand our services are so highly and rigidly structured that the Spirit seems to have very little or virtually no control in these celebration gatherings in praise of Christ our Lord. On the other hand, their services are so loosely and simply structured, if structured at all, that the Spirit is clearly in complete control. Indeed in our services it is sometimes difficult to say whether the Spirit is really present, while in theirs, it is so powerfully and patently obvious that He is, one does not need to ask.

To Paul's confident affirmation that, "where the Spirit of the Lord is there is freedom" (2 Corinthians 3:17), one must further add: And where there is freedom, there is also joy—"joy in the Holy Spirit" (Romans 14:17). And if in fact: "Where the Spirit of the Lord is there is freedom," and where there is freedom, there is joy, then one would also necessarily have to say, in terms of true Christian worship, that: where the Spirit of the Lord is not, there is bondage, and bondage in any form, let alone in matters of the Spirit, produces anything but joy.

When we structure the service so routinely and rigidly and feel such a deep and unswerving obligation to the written order of service and subscribe most faithfully to the view that the length of the service should be firmly and finally set and determined by cultural norms of convenience, rather than the influence and direction of the Holy Spirit, we in effect leave little or no room for the working and moving of the Spirit with and among the worshipers in those free and spontaneous expressions of sharing that always contribute significantly to a worship experience of ineffable, incredible, and inspiring joy.

To be sure there needs to be some order of service. Chaos or confusion is never part of the Spirit's plan for worship. But the order of service should always be a means to the all-important end in Christian worship—the realization of a truly joyful, spiritual experience one with another and with Christ. Thus the service should always be subject to the will and direction of the Holy Spirit, the only One who is divinely qualified to make Christian worship in any context an authentic and deeply fulfilling spiritual experience.

Indeed the Holy Spirit is the source of joy in Christian worship. When the order of service therefore as given in the bulletin becomes not a means to an end but an end in itself, when it is so faithfully adhered to that there is no opportunity for the free and spontaneous moving of the Spirit, and when it is so efficiently organized and timed for the convenience of members so that they would not be late for their next commitment, then to all intents and purposes the Holy Spirit is virtually stifled out of the service.

The Spirit, needless to say, functions best in an atmosphere of full freedom. We cannot on the one hand invite and invoke His presence in the service and on the other hand impose such rigid restrictions and limitations that He in essence is really not free to be the Spirit of Christ in the service. Thus Paul warns the Thessalonian Christians: "Do not quench the Holy Spirit" (1 Thessalonians 5:17). We quench the Spirit when we firmly deny Him the right and freedom to work, unhindered, within and among us. The Holy Spirit cannot and must not be bound. He must be completely free to guide, lead, and influence the service in whatever way or ways He deems fit and necessary for the greatest fulfillment, inspiration, and joy to all the worshipers.

The exciting thing about African worship is its loose order or structure, whether written or unwritten, so that the Holy Spirit is fully free to enhance the order and thus the worship as a whole, if He so wills, by making His presence clearly and powerfully felt and known through the spontaneous sharing or contributions, in whatever way and by whomever He may move or lead to be instruments of inspiration and joy in worship. And this seems to be the common expectation and anticipation whenever the congregation gathers for worship.

Invariably in the United Methodist churches I have pastored, churches for the most part with very few if any minorities, I would from time to time have different, primarily African Christian groups, musical and missionary, come and inspire us with their unique and excitingly joyful ways of worshiping and praising God, to expose the congregations to a variety of authentic forms and styles of Christian worship. Generally most of the groups were well received, some enthusiastically, others politely.

Almost always, however, there would be voices of protest and disapproval. to some the music was too loud, and for them, loud music is highly inappropriate in a church. To others it sounded just like rock music and rock 'n roll music has no place in a worship service. And of course there were those who complained that the service was too long. A few times members were so offended that I was asked by church leaders not to bring these groups back. On one occasion in particular, a young woman in a joyfully ecstatic expression of praise, adoration, and gratitude to God, exuberantly danced down the aisle to the very inspirational, instrumental African music, with body swaying and arms and legs swinging vigorously in every direction to the glory of God and in the authentic, tribal African style. Some "pillar" members thought the dancing was obscene and threatened that if any such group came back, they would withdraw their membership from the church.

United Methodists, when they gather for worship, need to lighten up and loosen up so that the liberating presence and power of the Spirit can truly transform the service into an experience of authentic Christian celebration and joy.

4

The Cross in Conflict with Culture

Our privileged role as Christians is to be representatives or as Paul very accurately puts it "ambassadors of Christ" in this world, ever mindful of the fact that though we are in the world, we are not of the world. As ambassadors of Christ, we represent a Kingdom, the Kingdom of God, that is, whose value system is radically different from and in some respects diametrically opposed to the value systems of the kingdoms and the nations of this world. Our first obligation and responsibility therefore as ambassadors of Christ is to dutifully represent the best interests of the Kingdom we belong to, the Kingdom of God, and not those of the secular kingdom or state in which we currently reside or of which we are citizens. And we represent the divine Kingdom best when we faithfully and without compromise fulfill the will and word of Christ as His ambassadors in the secular state or kingdom of our citizenship and in the world. In practical terms therefore to be ambassadors of Christ is to do the will and word of Christ our King particularly as expressed and given in the Sermon on the Mount (Matthew: 5–7).

The Sermon on the Mount is in essence the summary code of the fundamental virtues and values instituted and prescribed by Christ for the new Kingdom of God that He came with the express mission and task to establish and inaugurate in this world—the core virtues and values that all

Christians with their first loyalty to the Kingdom of God as citizens must necessarily subscribe to and live by. The Sermon on the Mount, while it applies with special relevance and reference to all Christians, constitutes the most idealistic moral code of conduct that is universally applicable to all humanity. Its moral significance from a biblical perspective is, that on the level of Christian ethics, the rest of the New Testament is in reality an expansion, elaboration, and explanation of the core Christian virtues and values given in this Sermon.

Needless to say, this Sermon rises most impressively and idealistically to an ethical height quite beyond the reach or grasp in practical terms of any mortal. Thus the significance and power of "Christ in you." It is again a reminder that even with the best will and intention in the world, because of sinful human nature, we are unable on our own to consistently do the right and the good to realize our best potential. It is only the empowering "Christ in you" that enables us morally and spiritually to rise to our highest potential if we give Him the full right and freedom to exercise complete control over us.

Also the moral civil war within that we are continuously engaged in between the forces of good and evil, each striving to be the dominant influence in our lives, is not simply a personal, internal struggle with consequences confined exclusively within. This internal civil war is in fact integrally connected with the external moral struggle between the forces of good and evil that we encounter daily at every facet, level, and aspect of our culture, society, and world, in terms of our personal response to this external struggle. And the nature and effectiveness of our response are entirely determined by and dependent on the outcome of the battle within.

Again, if we live seriously, committed lives as Christians, conflict with the world and its system of values is inevitable, for the values of this world are often in radical contrast to Christian values: "Do not love the world or the things in the world. The love of the Father is not in those who love the world; for all that is in the world—the desire of the flesh, the desire of the eyes, the pride in riches—comes not from the Father but from the world. And the world and its desire are passing away, but those who do the will of God live forever" (1 John 2:15–17). "No one can serve two masters; for a slave will either hate the one and love the other, or be devoted to the one and despise the other. You cannot serve God and wealth" (Matthew 6:24).

The radical nature of this contrast and conflict between worldly values and Christian values finds its classic expression in the Cross. In the eternal cosmic moral war between the forces of good and evil, its most crucial, pivotal, and decisive battle in all history was fought on the Cross. The Cross was the place and point in this classic universal war between good and evil where God's greatest good and gift to humanity, Christ our Lord, met in cosmic conflict with man's greatest evil, the Crucifixion of the only sinless, perfect Person who ever lived—a Crucifixion that took place for no just reason or cause but only because, irony of ironies, Christ was the perfect personification of the highest and greatest good.

One of the two criminals crucified on the Cross with Christ said it best in reference to the perfect goodness of Christ: "One of the criminals who were hanged there kept deriding Him and saying, 'Are you not the Messiah? Save yourself and us.' But the other rebuked him, saying, 'Do you not fear God since you are under the same sentence of condemnation? And we indeed have been condemned justly, for we are getting what we deserve for our deeds, but this man has done nothing wrong' " (Luke 23:39–41). And it seemed, initially at any rate, that in this all-important cosmic conflict between the greatest good and the greatest evil, that evil had scored a most significant and conclusive victory and that the good had been crushed, crucified, and buried forever, but the third day dramatically, miraculously and triumphantly changed that for all time and eternity and guaranteed decisively that ultimately and always good will triumph over evil.

It convincingly confirmed that on the Cross Christ had finally and fully won the battle for the good, the right, and the truth for all time and that as a result, He and He alone possesses inexhaustible power and resources to help all those who qualify for them in their internal personal conflict with evil so that they too can confidently triumph over evil just as He did. As already noted, His triumphant victorious declaration after His Resurrection says it all: "All authority in heaven and on earth has been given to me. Go therefore and make disciples of all nations, baptizing them in the name of the Father and of the Son and of the Holy Spirit, and teaching them to obey everything I have commanded you. And remember I am with you always, to the end of the age" (Matthew 28:19–20).

What triumphed on the Cross was not simply the good but in fact and in particular, in terms of values and virtues, the highest and greatest good in all of life, divine and human, the good of Love. "And now faith, hope and love abide, these three, and the greatest of these is Love" (1 Corinthians 13:13). "No one has greater love than this to lay down one's life for one's friends" (John 15:13).

The third day is significant. God could certainly have made the Resurrection happen immediately after the burial or shortly thereafter, but He didn't—an important reminder to us that just as Christ's Resurrection and victory were not immediate, victory for us in some of our own personal, ongoing struggles with evil may not be immediate. Indeed it almost always will not be immediate. And it may not even be the third day or even the third year. But that is not the guarantee.

The absolute guarantee is not when the victory will come, but that the victory absolutely, unfailingly, even miraculously, will come. And while we are waiting for victory—in the heat and bitter intensity of the struggle—the other powerful and most reassuring guarantee is that He will always be there, struggling side by side with us: "And remember I am with you always, to the end of the age." What triumphant reassurance!

The radical nature of the difference between the values and fundamental principles that are at the heart and center of our faith and those of the world not only ensures that if we are faithful to Christ that conflict is inescapable, but in fact, and logically so, the more faithful we are, the bitter and sharper will the conflict be.

Thus Paul reminds Timothy: "Indeed all who want to live a godly life in Christ Jesus will be persecuted" (2 Timothy 3:12). And it is for this very reason that Christ in His farewell message to His disciples forewarned them that conflict with the world to the point of suffering was not simply a possibility but an absolute certainty: "I have told you all this so that in me you may find peace. In the world you will have suffering. But take heart! I have conquered the world" (John 16:33).

And Paul confirms that the real nature of this ongoing continuous conflict we are engaged in throughout life is not material or physical but moral and spiritual: "For our struggle is not against enemies of blood and flesh but against the rulers, against the authorities, against the cosmic powers of this present darkness against the spiritual forces of evil in the heavenly places" (Ephesians 6:12).

Consequently the weapons we need to wage this war and to do it successfully are necessarily spiritual ones—weapons only Christ can provide us with through His Holy Spirit: "Therefore take up the whole armor of God, so that you may be able to withstand on that evil day, and having done everything to stand firm. Stand therefore and fasten the belt of truth around your waist and put on the breastplate of righteousness. As shoes for your feet put on whatever will make you ready to proclaim the gospel of peace. With all of these take the shield of faith, with which you will be able to quench all the flaming arrows of the evil one. Take the helmet of salvation and the sword of the Spirit which is the word of God" (Eph. 6:13–17).

It is interesting and indeed quite revealing that in this spiritual "armor" provided for the Christian in one's ongoing battle with external evil all the weapons, save one, are weapons of defense. The one exception, the only weapon of offense is the Word of God, the sword of the Spirit. The clear message here is that evil, in particular external evil in society and in the world, cannot be effectively and decisively defeated if fought exclusively on the defensive level. Christians must not only be active participants but must also be in the forefront of this ongoing struggle with evil in all its multifarious manifestations and expressions in society and in the world if we are truly and consistently to be overcomers. Worthy of note too is the fact that with evil as entrenched and multifaceted as it is in all aspects, areas, and levels of culture and society, we are only given one weapon of offense—the Word of God, the Bible.

The simple but significant message in this regard is that the Bible is God's only multipurpose, all-sufficient weapon of offense against evil. Therefore, if used to its full potential, its incredible power can overcome, demolish, and destroy any evil in society and in the world, whatever be its type, nature, or magnitude.

Also of importance is the fact that Paul describes the Word of God as the sword of the Spirit. The point here is that if we are to be skillful in its use, we need to be instructed by the Holy Spirit. Only the Spirit is qualified to train us ably and competently in the use of this key indispensable weapon in our spiritual arsenal. If we try to use this weapon on our own without the necessary adequate training by the Spirit, chances are we will use it inefficiently and ineffectively and thus with unsatisfactory results. We must therefore enlist the Holy Spirit as our Guide and Instructor in the expert use of His sword, the Bible. What this means, in essence, is that the Bible should not only be read, but studied with much diligence and discipline and as often as we study it, our constant prayer should be for the Holy Spirit to guide us, not only in discerning and understanding the practical and spiritual truths of the Word but, most importantly, in faithfully and fearlessly applying these truths to all the various life situations and challenges that confront us from day to day.

The author of Hebrews also emphasizes the incredible, penetrating power of the Word of God in that when it is used expertly and skillfully and to its full potential, under the Spirit's guidance, of course, it is much sharper than a sword, even a double-edged sword, in its incisive precision and effectiveness: "Indeed the word of God is living and active, sharper than any two-edged sword, piercing until it divides soul from spirit, joints from marrow; it is able to judge the thoughts and intentions of the heart" (Heb. 4:12).

In the aggressive use of God's Word as the most potent spiritual weapon in our lifelong struggle against evil, we have the perfect example of no other than Christ our Lord, for no one used this indispensable instrument of moral and spiritual warfare more effectively and decisively than He did in His classic confrontation with the ultimate source of all evil, the Devil, in the wilderness temptations. Jesus countered each of the three temptations advanced by the Devil with the irrefutable and invincible Word of God. To the first temptation: "If you are the Son of God, command this stone to become a loaf of bread," Jesus answered on the authority of the divine Word: "'Scripture says, 'Man is not to live on bread alone' " (Luke 4:3–4). Then after showing him all the kingdoms of the world, the Devil next tempted Him thus: "To you I will give their glory and all this authority; for it has been given to me and I give it to anyone I please. If you then will worship me, it will be yours." Jesus's scriptural response was: "It is written, 'Worship the Lord your God and serve only him' " (Luke 46:8). Finally, the Devil took Him to the pinnacle of the temple in Jerusalem and tempted Him with this challenge: "If you are the Son of God, throw yourself down from here for it is written, 'He will command his angels concerning you to protect you and on their hands they will bear you up so that you will not dash your foot against a stone.' " Jesus' scriptural counter this time was: "It is said, 'Do not put the Lord your God to the test' " (Luke 4:9–12).

A most important objective of these temptations, therefore, is that this experience and example of Jesus are primarily for our benefit and advantage—to remind us, that is, that in our constant and inescapable struggle with evil in all its various forms and manifestations, we can always depend on the invincible power of the Word of God to give us both security and victory.

To use the Word of God, therefore, as a spiritual weapon of offense against evil means that we must apply the appropriate word, just as Jesus did to the different situations of evil we confront from time to time. And we must be aggressive in the use of the Word in the sense that we must be resolute and zealous in our practical application of the Word. Needless to say, to apply the Word practically, we must know the Word and know it well—thus again the primary value and necessity of Bible study in the life of the seriously committed Christian. It is when we know the Word well in the course of and as a result of Bible study that we, through the guiding power and influence of the Holy Spirit, acquire the expertise and skill in its practical use and application.

The awesome challenge, indeed the moral responsibility of the Christian in his or her continuous confrontation with evil at all levels of life in society and in the world, is, in the words of Paul, to "stand firm" (Eph. 6:13). Having been fully equipped for battle both defensively and offensively, we should "stand firm," and defiantly so, on the solid ground of justice, peace and love and be unyielding, unwavering, unrelenting and uncompromising in our confrontation with evil, bearing in mind always that some victories come quickly and other victories take a rather long time to achieve, and this is particularly so in the moral and spiritual realm.

Some battles are inevitably long primarily because of the nature of the evil, which may be so deeply entrenched that it is very difficult if not almost impossible to eradicate, the type of institutional evil that is generally and inherently found in, to use the biblical term, "principalities and powers" (Eph. 6:12). And when the battle is long and the foe formidable, there is a strong temptation even sometimes among the most faithful Christians, to waver and to compromise. A long battle also brings with it a greater likelihood of discouragement, disappointment, despair, even distrust among those united in the struggle against this particular evil. But it is precisely in these cases and circumstances that the Christian should "stand firm." In this connection the moral race, so to speak, is not a sprint but a marathon. "Then many will fall away and they will betray one another and hate one another. And many false prophets will arise and lead many astray. And because of the increase of lawlessness, the love of many will grow cold. But the one who endures to the end will be saved" (Matt. 24:10–12).

At the end of the wilderness temptations, the Devil, according to Luke, "departed from Him until an opportune time" (Luke 4:13). Again, the message here is primarily for our enlightenment, so that we may better understand how the Devil operates and realize how persistent and subtle his methods are. Thus the Christian should also "stand firm" because, as we saw in the case of Jesus, the Devil never gives up but keeps coming back and attacking again and again, with ever more sinister and subtle devices, particularly if it is an area in which we are very weak or vulnerable. Worthy of note in this regard is the fact that the Devil's strategy as he comes back in his repeated attacks on us, is that he does not come at any time, but at "opportune" times—the times, that is, when we are most vulnerable and likely to be very susceptible to his wily and devious charms. That is why we are given so many weapons of defense, as we have already noted, to enable us to be always on our guard. And our defense strategy needs to be organized by the Spirit, for we can never on our own have the most secure defense for an enemy as crafty as the Devil, that will completely eliminate the possibility of any unguarded moments. In this regard, Paul cautions us to be diligently aware of "the wiles of the devil" (Eph. 6:11).

This brings us to true reality in our everyday conflict with evil. Our imperfect sinful nature guarantees that Christian though we are, we cannot have such a perfectly personal moral defense system that it would absolutely ensure against any and all unguarded moments in our lives. That is not realistic even for the most dedicated, devoted, and disciplined Christian. The objective of our personal moral and spiritual defense strategy, therefore, under the guidance and direction of the Holy Spirit, is to keep such unguarded moments to the minimum. On this issue too, James's advice is both pertinent and practical: "Resist the devil and he will flee from you" (James 4:7). We can only successfully resist the Devil through the power of the Holy Spirit in us in His role as our Guide in our conflict with evil.

After Jesus triumphantly overcame these temptations, Luke reveals, most significantly, that, "Jesus filled with the power of the Spirit returned to Galilee and a report about him spread through all the surrounding country. He began to teach in their synagogue and was praised by everyone" (Luke 4:14–15). In principle, the same thing happens to us as happened to Christ when we successfully stand our ground in resisting the Devil—the victory energizes us spiritually with the result that we become newly "filled with the power of the Spirit." We are thus more zealously and passionately motivated to counter the evils in our society and to be fearless champions of justice, peace, and love for the welfare, and well-being of our fellow men and women, particularly the poor and powerless, the oppressed and the dispossessed in the community and in the world.

Little wonder then that the next crucial event in the life and ministry of Christ immediately after the temptations was His momentous visit to the synagogue in His hometown of Nazareth, where on the authority of the Word of God, He made this bold declaration:

The Spirit of the Lord is upon me, because he has anointed me to bring good news to the poor. He has sent me to proclaim release to the captives and recovery of sight to the blind, to let the oppressed go free, to proclaim the year of the Lord's favor." And he rolled up the scroll, gave it back to the attendant and sat down. The eyes of all in the synagogue were fixed on him. Then he began to say to them: "Today this scripture has been fulfilled in your hearing." All spoke well of him and were amazed at the gracious words that came from his mouth (Luke 4:18–21).

The Christian should indeed take a firm and unequivocal stand against all forms of evil in society, for that is an integral part of our assigned mission and mandate in the world as ambassadors of Christ and as disciples of our Lord. And in the inspired and inspiring example of Christ given here, we must not and indeed cannot compromise on those oppressive evils and evil systems that callously and brutally debase, dehumanize, or destroy our fellow men and women, persons of priceless worth who as God's children bear His divine image indelibly on them. All evils are evils primarily because of the harm or hurt they unjustly cause in one way or another, either directly or indirectly, immediately or ultimately to fellow human beings. As Christians, therefore, our solemn moral mission in our struggle against evil in society is to diligently and determinedly work to reform, dismantle, or destroy those systems and structures that result in or are responsible for the oppression, the dehumanization, or the unjust elimination of the individual person or a certain group, race, or class of people.

In this regard, Christians in South Africa and to a certain extent Christians around the world who joined them in their long, painful and bitter struggle against the despicable and diabolical evil of apartheid need to be highly commended for staying the course. It was a fight which, because it was so long and because the evil was so deeply and pervasively entrenched in all areas and aspects of South African life, including principally all levels of the political and governmental structures within the country, must have seemed at many points along the way a frustratingly fruitless, endless, even hopeless moral commitment and challenge. And inevitably, because it was so long, disappointment, disillusionment, and discouragement were frequent but unwelcome companions on this difficult road to liberation, freedom, and victory. But because the faithful Christians of South Africa never wavered in their passionate zeal and love for Christ; because they firmly believed in the just nature of their struggle; because, in spite of setbacks, government intransigence, and brutal oppression, they faithfully persevered, because they knew the monstrous nature of the evil they were fighting and knew that it was one, be the consequences what they may, on which they could not comprise; because they believed and knew that the God of their faith never leaves His oppressed people in the bondage of oppression forever; because above all they believed in the power of prayer and in a God of absolute justice, freedom, and righteousness—the miracle happened! An incredible victory was achieved over the hideously evil forces of apartheid!

While every Christian is called as an integral and necessary part of his or her mission in life to challenge the evil systems and structures in society and external evil in general, wherever it is found, realistically no one Christian can seriously, effectively, and practically engage in moral combat with all the various manifestations and expressions of evil that confront us continuously—and no one Christian is expected to do that. To try to fight on so many different moral fronts at the same time can indeed prove to be counterproductive, particularly in the case of those evils that are deeply entrenched and would necessarily therefore require and involve a very lengthy moral engagement. In the attempt to be effective in combating all evils, admirable and commendable as this may seem, one is likely to end up not being effective in any. It is definitely not the most responsible and productive use of one's limited time, skills, and resources.

As a Christian who is seriously committed to constructively combating evil, one has to necessarily choose one's battles. The question then that one is inevitably confronted with is: What determines which battle(s) one chooses? The simple answer is that if the Holy Spirit is indeed in full and complete control of our lives, He will lead us naturally and unerringly into those moral encounters where we will be the most effective. We are limited also by the spiritual gifts we have been blessed with. And the one is related to the other in the sense that the same Spirit that controls and determines what external moral evils we challenge in society is the very Spirit that equips us with the spiritual gifts we have been given to be used in the service of the Kingdom of God and to the good and well-being of our fellow men and women, particularly the poor, the powerless, and the oppressed. Then too our professional or job skills and experience may give us a clue as to what situation of social and moral evils we must fearlessly confront. And of course where we live in terms of the particular community, state or country may not be simply accidental or a decision exclusively of our own making, but rather the fact that God has deliberately placed us there to be a witness for Him and the Christian cause against the corrosive moral, social, political, and or economic evils that afflict that particular community, state or country.

The fearless and formidable seventh century (B.C.) prophet Jeremiah, one of the most powerful, prophetic voices in Jewish history, was directly called and chosen by God at that particular point in the history of Israel to challenge and confront both rulers and ruled with the abominable and atrocious evils that were sadly but surely destroying both people and nation. After some initial hesitation and reluctance on account of his youth, Jeremiah responded positively to the irresistible call and claim of God on his life.

Now the word of the Lord came to me saying, "Before I formed you in the womb I knew you, and before you were born I consecrated you; I appointed you a prophet to the nations." Then I said, "Ah, Lord God! Truly I do not know how to speak, for I am only a boy." But the Lord said to me, "Do not say, I am only a boy, for you shall go to all to whom I send you, and you shall speak whatever I command you.

Do not be afraid of them, for I am with you to deliver you," says the Lord.

Then the Lord put out his hand and touched my mouth and the Lord said to me, "Now I have put my words in your mouth. See today I appoint you over nations and kingdoms, to pluck up and to put down, to destroy and to overthrow, to build and to plant" (Jer. 1:4–10).

Even after responding affirmatively to the call, as many who have thus responded to the divine call have subsequently discovered, the internal struggle was not over for Jeremiah:

O Lord, you have enticed me and I was enticed; you have overpowered me and you have prevailed. I have become a laughing stock all day long: everyone mocks me. For whenever I speak, I must cry out. I must shout, "Violence and destruction!" For the word of the Lord has become for me a reproach and derision all day long. If I say "I will not mention him or speak any more in his name," then within me there is something like a burning fire shut up in my bones; I am weary with holding it in and I cannot (Jer. 20:7–9).

With the inner power, conviction, and courage that always comes with the divine call, Jeremiah boldly, bitterly, and blisteringly attacked the many evils to which his fellow compatriots had so easily succumbed, to their own moral, spiritual, economic, and political ruin. Because God was not in control of their lives, they did not possess the spiritual and moral power within to overcome these destructive evils, but were instead overcome by them:

For from the least to the greatest of them everyone is greedy for unjust gain; and from prophet to priest everyone deals falsely. They have treated the wound of my people carelessly saying, "Peace, peace, when there is no peace." They acted shamefully, they committed abominations; yet they were not ashamed, they did not know how to blush. Therefore, they shall fall among those who fall; at the time that I punish them they shall be overthrown, says the Lord (Jer. 6:13–15).

Jeremiah scathingly denounced their callous and depraved hypocrisy in his prophetic warnings from the temple:

For if you truly amend your ways and your doings, if you truly act justly one with another, if you do not oppress the alien, the orphan and the widow, or shed innocent blood in this place and if you do not go after other gods to your own hurt, then I will dwell with you in this place, in the land that I give of old to your ancestors for ever and ever. Here you are, trusting in deceptive words to no avail. Will you steal, murder, commit adultery, swear falsely, make offerings to Baal and go after other gods that you have not known, and then come and stand before me in this house, which is called by my name and say "We are safe!"—only to go on doing all these abominations? Has this house which is called by my name become a den of robbers in your sight! (Jer. 7:5–11).

And on both King and people, divine judgment was pronounced because of their corrupt and evil ways:

Therefore, thus says the Lord, concerning King Jehoiakim of Judah, he shall have no one to sit upon the throne of David and his dead body shall be cast out to the heat by day and the frost by night. And I will punish him and his offspring and his servants for their iniquity; I will bring on them and on the inhabitants of Jerusalem and on the people of Judah all the disasters with which I have threatened them, but they would not listen (Jer. 36:30–31).

The most fearless firebrand of the Old Testament prophets, Amos of Tekoa, was also called by God from his occupation to be His prophetic witness and voice at that particular

time—eighth century (B.C.)— in the history of the Northern
Kingdom of Israel, even though he was from the Southern
Kingdom of Judah. This was a time of great prosperity for
both kingdoms, due primarily and coincidentally to the long,
stable and materially progressive reigns of King Uzziah in
Judah (792–740 B.C.) and King Jeroboam in Israel (793–753
B.C.) But a time of great national prosperity almost always
brings with it a time of greater moral depravity. Needless to
say, and tragically so, Israel and Judah, in particular the former, were no exception to this rule. Unfortunately, the out-
ward glitz, glitter, and glamour of a prosperous people were
not only lulling both nations into a false sense of security,
but they were also covering up a state of moral and spiritual
ill-health that was fundamentally rotten to the core. The
tragic evil of this great prosperity for both nations, more
so the Northern Kingdom, particularly for the chosen and
covenant people of God, was that the wealth was not evenly
distributed and shared among all classes of people. Indeed,
the revolting and appalling irony was that in the midst of
and in spite of this incredible wealth and prosperity, the poor
masses were not only getting poorer, but horror of horrors,
they were getting poorer precisely because the callous, heart-
less, and rapacious rich were mercilessly and oppressively
increasing their wealth by greedily fleecing the poor.

And what was even worse and more reprehensible was
that they were doing it without the slightest evidence of guilt
or shame. They were so consumed by the obscene passion
for wealth and had become such slaves to riches that they
were prepared to go to any and all extremes. however immoral and degrading, to realize their filthy, financial objective. No means was off-limits or could be considered too
sacred to use towards their one and only monetary end. For-
saking the one true God, the only god they now worshiped
with passionate devotion and dedication was the god of

money and materialism. For them it was not simply the case of worshiping the creature more than the creator, rather it was the case of worshiping only the creature of comfort, wealth, and luxury. A covenant people called and chosen by God to be a spiritual light to the peoples and nations of the world, to be a moral model and standard for other nations, had become so grossly immoral and in certain respects even worse than some of the neighboring nations, that she thus forfeited her unique right and privilege to be God's chosen light to the world. Israel had truly failed and failed most miserably and unforgivably on the most important moral criterion that should clearly distinguish the people of God from the other peoples of the world—the compassionate care, justice and equality for the poor, the oppressed, the alien, the stranger.

This was the sad and sickening spiritual state and situation that afflicted God's chosen people, resulting in the divine, prophetic call to Amos to leave his home in Tekoa in the south and go to Bethel in the north to confront, condemn, and castigate the Northern Kingdom for its gross moral and social evils. Interestingly enough, Amos was not a prophet by profession, but because most of the professional prophets were themselves guiltily and deeply involved in the very social and moral evils they were called to condemn, this necessarily rendered them incapable and ill-qualified to truly fulfill the prophetic role. They were in essence false prophets. Amos's economic circumstances, while by no means destitute, clearly classified him among the poor in Judah. His occupation was that of a shepherd and "a dresser of sycamore trees," the fruit of which was generally eaten by the poorer class of people. "Then Amos answered Amaziah (priest of Bethel). 'I am no prophet nor a prophet's son; but I am an herdsman and a dresser of sycamore trees, and the Lord took me from following the flock and the Lord said to me, 'Go prophesy to my people Israel' " (Amos 7:14–15).

The nature of Amos's calling is a reminder that we do not have to be professionally called to the ministry to stand boldly and bear public and prophetic witness against the prevailing evils and sins of our society. We are called as Christians regardless of what work we do or who we are to bear witness in word and deed against the corrosive and cancerous evils that afflict our community, our society, our country, and our world. It is highly unlikely that Amos was just chosen at random or by accident from all the shepherds in Judah to fulfill this prophetic mission. Rather the clear and confident assumption is that Amos was called precisely and primarily because he must have been continuously in the course of his occupation as "herdsman and a dresser of sycamore trees," bearing witness in one form or another against the social and economic evils of his time and society. Thus when the call did come, Amos was eminently prepared and qualified by God's standards for the prophetic task and challenge divinely assigned to him. And coming from among the poor, he obviously experienced at first hand and was well acquainted with the widespread and oppressive consequences on the desperate and destitute poor, of the greedy and grasping practices of the wealthy. In his passionate, dynamic and fiery prophetic style, Amos fervently and fearlessly championed the cause of the poor, the powerless, the dispossessed, and the downtrodden in his bold and withering attacks on the corrupt and criminal atrocities of the wealthy. With his absolute, divine, 'Thus says the Lord!' authority, his relentless clarion call in his stern prophetic voice for true justice and righteousness thundered throughout the length and breadth of Israel and Judah:

Thus says the Lord! For three transgressions of Israel and for four, I will not revoke the punishment; because they sell the righteous for silver, and the needy for a pair of sandals. They who trample the head of the poor into the dust of the earth, and push the afflicted out of the way; father and son go into the same girl, so that my holy name is profaned (Amos 2:6–7).

Therefore, because you trample on the poor and take from them levies of grain, you have built houses of hewn stones; but you shall not live in them. You have planted pleasant vineyards; but you shall not drink their wine (Amos 5:11).

But let justice roll down like waters and righteousness like an everflowing stream (Amos 5:24).

Hear this you that trample on the needy, and bring to ruin the poor of the land, saying, "When will the new moon be over, so that we may sell grain; and the sabbath, so that we may offer wheat for sale? We will make the ephah small and the shekel great, and practise deceit with false balances, buying the poor for silver and the needy for a pair of sandals, and selling the sweepings of the wheat (Amos 8:4–6).

And it was the prophetic role in South Africa so inspiringly and courageously exercised by Archbishop Desmond Tutu, Rev. Beyers Naude, Rev. Frank Chikane, Rev. Alan Boesak, former Presiding Methodist Bishop Stanley Mogoba, and countless others that played such a leading part in the final and complete destruction of apartheid.

In the New South Africa, religious leaders continue to raise their prophetic voices against the social, economic, and moral evils that afflict South African society. Their call for moral renewal in South Africa resulted in the Moral Summit of October 1998, organized by the National Religious Leaders Forum and chaired by Presiding Methodist Bishop Mvume Dandala. The summit, attended by President Nelson Mandela and other political leaders, produced a Moral Code of Conduct that all participants of the summit had to sign, implying obviously that if moral renewal is to come to the country as a whole, it has to start at the top. The Moral

Summit was the initiative of the National Religious Leaders Forum (NRLF), a body that was set up about a year ago in order to find a common response to President Mandela's appeal for moral renewal: "The real hard work will be to analyse together the causes of our present moral problems and the actions which need to be taken to change the situation."

We have been called as Christians to do good wherever we are and in whatever circumstances we may find ourselves, not only destructively by dismantling evil systems but also constructively by practicing genuine deeds of Christian love. And Christian love is not authentic Christian love if it is not sacrificial love. Sacrifice in one sense or another, in one way or another, needs always to be an integral and necessary part of Christian love. Indeed it is sacrifice that truly gives Christian love its most distinctive and unique characteristic. And sacrifice plays such a central part of Christian love because the sacrifice of Christ on the Cross was the most convincing expression of His matchless divine love for all humanity. Thus our brothers and sisters in the Methodist Church of Southern Africa were not only actively working over the years for the destruction and demise of the oppressive evil system of apartheid, but with equal and committed Christian zeal, they were also doing good constructively in their many practical expressions of authentic Christian love—love that had at its very center the principal Christian characteristic of sacrifice. What was most revealing and deeply touching to us during our mission trips to Southern Africa was the sacrificial commitment we witnessed in many churches and individual Christians in terms of their involvement in programs and projects within the church and community—in particular the community soup kitchens sponsored by the churches. These were very poor and destitute communities and the meal provided was very simple—in many cases just a bowl of soup—but even when many of its important needs were still unmet, e.g. repairs to the building, the church, obviously at great sacrifice, kept the program going because for many in that community who came to the soup kitchen, that would be their only meal for the day. And many of the volunteer help for these programs are church members, who although they can ill afford to, because of their large families, would miss a day's work from time to time to help to feed the hungry in their community.

Their deep spirituality rooted in their abiding and abundant love for Christ inspires and motivates them to practice a quality of Christian love that is commendably sacrificial. They could easily have discontinued the program because of other pressing financial needs within the church, but for them it was more important to ensure that a hungry child in the community had at least one meal a day than attending to their own needs as a church. To them too it was important that the light of Christian compassion and love shine brightly in the community in terms of meeting basic and primary human needs, "so that others may see your good works and glorify your Father who is in heaven" (Matt 5:16). Certainly when the church's light of compassion and love shines in such a practical and exemplary way in the community, it becomes also a light of evangelism, bringing more people to the church and to the Lord.

In one of the churches with a soup kitchen in which one could clearly see that significant repairs were needed on the building, a church leader, when asked when the church was planning to do the repairs, shared in an answer that was very typical of the unquestioning and unwavering faith and dependence on God that we were so deeply impressed with throughout our visit, that it was God's house and when He was ready for the repairs to be done, He would provide the necessary funds. God, he confidently shared, had faithfully come through for them so many times before for various church needs that he was not in the least worried about it.

Indeed the whole issue of poverty and the many and mammoth social evils that it inevitably gives rise to have assumed such a major, even alarming role in the life of rural black communities and townships that the churches, most commendably, have found it necessary to come together in a very exemplary ecumenical effort to address the problem. In referring to this dreaded plague of poverty that ruins the lives and dreams of so many black South Africans, particularly the youth, the Bishop of the Anglican Church in Pretoria, the Right Rev. Jo Seoka, who assumed office in 1998, and who sees his primary mission as bishop as that "of restoring dignity to the blind, the lame, the cripples, the beggars, the poor, the prostitutes and all the other outcasts of his time" pointedly observes "The frightening thing is that for so many of these people, life no longer seems to have any meaning at all."

Thus the War on Poverty Forum was convened in August 1998 by the South African Council of Churches to seriously and practically work together across denominational lines and in the true spirit of Christian unity to address the tragic impact of poverty on the lives of individuals, families, and communities. Very importantly, this ecumenical gathering somewhat prophetically acknowledged "that the role of the Church community is to ensure that the voices of the poor reverberate in the halls of public policy." In more concrete terms the churches have been instrumental in the establishment of the Young Christian Workers National Manifesto of Demands of Casual Workers, a manifesto that calls primarily "for job security, proper working conditions, and a living wage," and in the National Youth Policy, which the National Youth Commission presented to President Mandela in Capetown in 1998 as the hopes and dreams of the country's youth, who make up about 40 percent of South Africa's population.

In regard to the oppressive poverty in most black communities, the inspiring hope is that though poor in material resources, particularly in the rural areas, they are incredibly rich in spirit, in that vibrant, dynamic, community spirit, that is, which binds them so closely to each other and gives them all such a strong sense of solidarity, identity, and responsibility for each other as if they are all members of one large extended family.

It is that unique, authentic African spirit that they affectionately call *ubuntu*. *Time* magazine in its focus issue on Africa (March 30, 1998) titled, "Africa Rising" defines *ubuntu* in the following terms: "There is a word we heard over and over in Africa: *ubuntu*. It's different in every dialect but the meaning is always roughly the same: a complex, highly nuanced precept governing the way individuals relate to the community. *Ubuntu* is the organizing principle of the African mind, defining the pre-eminence of the interests of the community over the individual, the duties and responsibilities the individual owes the community, the obligation of the individual to share what he has with the community."

Closely linked in spirit and in practice with the inspiring and unifying tradition of *ubuntu* is the South African concept of *Masakhane* (we build together). The great idea of *Masakhane* as a campaign to mobilize and motivate the nation as a whole to work together at every level, including every sector and segment of the population in rebuilding a new apartheid-free South Africa, began with President Mandela's urgent call and challenge to the nation at Marconi Beam, a settlement near Cape Town, to put into practice the principles of self-help and self-sacrifice, the spirit of unity and togetherness, for the greater good of the nation, as he formally launched the national project and program of *Masakhane*.

In this essentially grassroots movement with an annual National Focus Week, the churches, needless to say, have played and continue to play a very vital and visible role:

The concept of *Masakhane* is derived from the African tradition of cooperative social responsibility. The central theme of the Campaign is that the nation must mobilize the power of the people to overcome the legacy of apartheid: poverty, crime, corruption, inequality and underdevelopment.

Some churches marched for peace and against poverty and crime, in addition to taking up collections of food and clothing for the poor. Churches are an important tool in any effort to rebuild the nation, said provincial campaign coordinators. And recent events such as the Moral Summit and the Jobs Summit confirm this. Coordinators said churches represent a significant constituency in society and through their grassroots network can promote *Masakhane* as part of every citizen's responsibility.

Christian love that is truly and genuinely sacrificial is not preoccupied or consumed exclusively with one's own interests, concerns, goals and needs. Rather it is one that reaches out constantly, continuously, ceaselessly to others—one that pursues relentlessly the interests, needs, the welfare, and well-being of others, even when it is not convenient to do so. It is this quality in Christian love that gives it the power to triumph over any and all obstacles. Its power and motivation spring primarily from within, which explains why it is invincible and irrepressible. In other words it is fully and firmly anchored in one's faith. Indeed it is the most convincing and concrete expression of the reality and authenticity of one's faith.

Authentic Christian love speaks in an ultimate sense of the sacrifice of Christ, the sacrifice of His life on the Cross for all humanity as proof of His eternal love:

This is my commandment that you love one another as I have loved you. No one has greater love than this, to lay down one's life for one's friends. You are my friends if you do what I command you" (John 15:12–14).

We know love by this, that he laid down his life for us—and we ought to lay down our lives for one another (1 John 3:16).

Christian love cannot be fully and clearly understood apart from the Cross. Indeed no aspect of the Christian faith could be understood without the Cross, but in terms of Christian love, it is virtually impossible to truly conceive of it, to really comprehend it, to genuinely experience it, and to adequately apply it with no integral or central connection to the Cross. It is the Cross that gives Christian love its transforming power, its transcendent hope, and its triumphant joy. It is the Cross that indelibly imprints upon Christian love its unique identity and gives it that persistent and persevering spirit to prevail. It is the Cross that gives Christian love the capacity to heal divisions and the endurance to strive ceaselessly and relentlessly towards real unity. It is the Cross that gives Christian love the courage to face all challenges and obstacles without fear and to be patient in the struggle until victory is won. It is the Cross that continuously inspires and motivates Christian love to break down all barriers and boundaries between all cultures, classes, races, and nationalities of people and to recognize that all peoples of the world, created as we are in the image of God, stand on the same common ground of equality before God as persons of priceless worth and value. It is the Cross that makes Christian love confront all forms and expressions of evil and work strenuously and tirelessly for true peace and justice.

In very clear, categorical terms, Jesus emphasized to His disciples the central role of the Cross in true Christian discipleship. In fact as Jesus sees it and spells it out, the role of the Cross for one who would like to be His disciple is not simply central—rather it is indispensable: "Then he said to them all, "If any want to become my followers, let them deny themselves and take up their cross daily and follow me'" (Luke 9:23). "Whoever does not carry the cross and follow me cannot be my disciple" (Luke 14:27).

Thus to be a disciple of Christ, on His terms not ours, means first and foremost, to embrace the discipline of the Cross, with all the sacrifice which that implies, involves, and demands. What Jesus was saying to His disciples, in other words, was that since the Cross was central and an absolute necessity in His life and mission for the redemption of all humanity, there is definitely no way that anyone could be His disciple and avoid, escape, or disregard the cross—one's own personal cross, that is, in terms of the demanding, sacrificial responsibilities that necessarily come with bearing one's own cross, the most primary of which is the sacrificial responsibility of authentic Christian love.

Because the Cross was central in the life and mission of Christ, the Cross and its sacrificial responsibilities must also be central in the life and mission of the disciple, for as He pointedly reminded them, "servants are not greater than their master nor are messengers greater than the one who sent them" (John 13:16). And if the Cross is indeed a central fact of the disciple's life, then the practical application of the Cross cannot be a periodic or haphazard commitment. The discipline of the Cross must necessarily be a daily, practical exercise. Only when we fulfill the sacrificial responsibilities of our faith that come with taking up our cross and doing so as a daily, continuous commitment of our lives, only then do we truly qualify to be the disciples of Christ, as prescribed and specified by our Lord Himself.

On Christ's terms, therefore, love must be the sacrificial way of life for the Christian, one that he or she is always, daily, continuously engaged in. In the circumstances one's mission, in essence and for all practical purposes, is to let one's light of sacrificial love so shine in the community and in the world that, "others would see your goodness and glorify your Father who is in heaven" (Matt. 5:16).

Paul challenged the Christians in Rome: "I appeal to you therefore, brothers and sisters, by the mercies of God to present your bodies as a living sacrifice, holy and acceptable to God, which is your spiritual worship. Do not be conformed to this world but be transformed by the renewing of your minds, so that you may discern what is the will of God—what is good and acceptable and perfect" (Rom. 12:1–2). It is only true, authentic Christian love that has the power to inspire us to give ourselves, our whole being, unconditionally and unresevedly to God, mind, body and soul, to be used as living instruments of sacrifice in His cause and for His service to the welfare and well-being of our fellow men and women, in particular, the poor and powerless in society and in the world.

In an affluent society, it is difficult, to say the least, for Christians to know what sacrifice in biblical terms is and means. In a culture of plenty, such as ours, where we have so much of everything material but so little of anything spiritual, where the life we pursue passionately is a life of comfort, not a life of compassion, where our primary preoccupation is with our own personal welfare and well-being, not the welfare and well-being of others, where we always have much time for self but very little time for others, and where love means for the most part what I can get, not what I can give, sacrifice, particularly as the New Testament understands it, is not a term one hears much about in Christian circles and is certainly not a popular practice in Christian experience.

In a culture and society that cares little for sacrifice, except if it is for one's own good and well-being, sacrifice as the biblical norm of forgoing one's own good for the greater good and benefit of others is extremely rare. Unfortunately, this cultural self-preoccupation as a guiding principle or way of life that denigrates and disregards sacrifice for others has exercised a disturbing impact and influence on the Church in general, with the result that even Christians seem for the most part to live as if they are more influenced by their culture than by their faith, in a general disregard of the biblical norm and standard of sacrificial love and commitment for the good of others. Thus the sacrifice Christians in our culture practice, if they practice any at all, seems more closely akin to the sacrifice our secular society practices, a sacrifice for one's own personal good rather than the authentic Christian ideal of sacrifice for the welfare of others.

Sacrificial Christian love of the cultural variety is not only a love that is expressed mostly for one's own benefit, but when it is expressed to and for others, it is generally more a matter of convenience than one of biblical principle and consistency—one does it when it is convenient for one to do so. Christian love as is practiced in our affluent society and culture is not for the most part Christian love with the Cross at its center, but rather Christian love with the culture at its center. Thus again the relevance of Paul's warning to the Christians in Rome: "Do not be conformed to this world" (Rom. 12:12). And to the Philippian Christians, he spells out the practical application of authentic, sacrificial Christian love:

Do nothing from selfish ambition or conceit, but in humility regard others as better than yourselves. Let each of you look not to your own interests but to the interests of others. Let the same mind be in you that was in Christ Jesus who though he was in the form of God, did not regard equality with God as something to be exploited, but emptied himself, taking the form of a slave being born in human likeness. And being found in human form, he humbled himself and became obedient to the point of death even death on a cross (Phil. 2:3–8).

Conclusion

This critical and challenging time in human history is also a critical and challenging time in the history of United Methodism in this country. The United Methodist Church is at a crucial crossroads. We can either, like our sister churches in Southern Africa and in Africa as a whole, truly make our Church the Church in which Jesus is indeed Lord, the Church of the Cross, that is, by making Christ and His mission our absolute first priority, in deed more than word, and so reverse our thirty-year continuous numerical decline; or, complacently, we can embrace the status quo, and let the Church continue to be the Church of our culture, one in which, in practical terms, the culture not the Cross, the culture and not Christ, is the dominant influence, a Church in other words that is "conformed to this world" and thus cannot transform it, and a Church therefore that will continue to experience an irreversible decline in both numbers and moral and spiritual influence.

For the beginning of this new century to be also for United Methodism a new beginning in terms of substantial and significant numerical growth, it means that the spiritual transformation of the Church as a whole, again more in deed than word, needs to be our number one priority, for spiritual growth is the biblical prerequisite and precondition to numerical and other growth

Like the Church in Africa, ours must be not simply a Sunday faith, as for the most part it seems to be, but a daily faith. The power of the Church in Africa is in the dedicated lives of ordinary Christians who are forever sharing their faith and joyfully living their faith as a daily sacrificial commitment and experience in spite of the difficult struggles and challenges they often have to endure. For them the Cross, not culture, is the primary daily influence on their lives: "'If any want to become my followers, let them deny themselves and take up their cross daily and follow me" (Luke 9:23).

Not only do they live their faith daily, they live it passionately, which reflects the depth of their commitment and conviction to Christ as Lord. One is never in doubt as to whether Christ and His mission are first priority in their lives. They talk about their Lord "in season and out of season" with great, unabashed enthusiasm.

Cultural influences tend generally to make United Methodists in this country rather casual and lukewarm about their faith. If our faith is in fact the central and dominant conviction in our lives, we need indeed to be passionate about it. We cannot transform others if we ourselves are not transformed and live as if we are. "I know your works; you are neither cold nor hot. I wish that you were either cold or hot. So because you are lukewarm, and neither cold or hot, I am about to spit you out of my mouth" (Rev. 3:15).

The faith of African Christians has such depth primarily because it is rooted and grounded in the Word of God. Prayer and Bible study constitute the foundation pillars of their spiritual lives. Their thorough knowledge of the Bible coupled with their personal commitment to Christ as Lord inspires in them a dedication to do the Word—to, in other words, use the Bible as a practical guide to all areas of their daily lives and living. What makes a decisive, dramatic difference in ministry and contributes significantly to the vibrant, dynamic spiritual life of the churches is the quality of the lay leadership. From all appearances, leaders are chosen primarily because of their exemplary, practical faith and spiritual commitment, and not simply because they are available or are unwilling to relinquish the power their position gives them. Most either lead prayer and Bible study groups or are very active in them and by so doing inspire faithful devotion in the members.

In some of our churches, leaders rarely attend the Sunday worship service, let alone take an active part in the spiritual life of the congregation. Most importantly, if our churches are to be transformed, we need not just leaders but transformed leaders in all positions of leadership. In this regard it is most revealing indeed that the UMC Connectional Process Team, the thirty-eight-member body "charged by the 1996 General Conference with guiding, promoting and managing the transformational direction for the denomination," identified "lack of spiritual leadership by both clergy and laity" as the primary reason preventing the United Methodist Church from achieving its central purpose of making disciples of Jesus Christ.

Fortunately there are some positive signs of hope. The General Council of Ministries, in its 1998 document, "Fulfilling Christ's Mission in the Life of the UMC," defined its mission in terms of a central focus on fulfilling the biblical mandate of making disciples of Jesus Christ. "Agencies are asked to invite and nurture people in spiritual growth centered on Scripture and our Wesleyan heritage, and develop lay and clergy leaders empowered by the Holy Spirit to lead the Church in spiritual transformation and service.

"Agencies are further urged to share the Gospel of Christ in a variety of ways; practice hospitality, celebrate differences, build a Christlike community; practice collaborative decision making; communicate effectively and compassionately God's movement throughout the Church and the world; speak prophetically to the realities of many cultures; work toward Christian unity; and strengthen interreligious relationships."

The Connectional Process Team, referred to above, in its draft proposal in fulfillment of its mandate from General Conference (1996) emphasized that the spiritual direction of the church should be its "primary focus": "The Team hopes a new General Conference can become a connecting point where UM's around the globe meet at a common table for the purpose of considering and celebrating our common doctrinal heritage and our mission and ministries as disciples who are part of a new world congregation. The primary focus would be on spiritual transformation rather than legislative and administrative matters."

It is significant, and hearteningly so, that in both of these general agencies of the church the consensus is that in order for the United Methodist Church to realize its greatest potential in terms of global mission as the Church of Jesus Christ, a spiritual focus is a prime necessity.

A further example of this hopeful trend for the future of United Methodism in this country is that a similar conclusion has been reached in the New England Conference of the Church. Under the resourceful episcopal leadership of Bishop Susan Hassinger, in the five critical issues that the 1998 Annual Conference adopted to realize its vision for the mission of Christ in New England, spiritual life is the number one priority, followed by Evangelism and Church Growth. The mission statement reads: "Our Mission as the New England Conference is to equip, connect and support local, regional and global ministries to make disciples of Jesus Christ and to serve all in His name."

And according to Bishop Ray Owen (San Antonio), one of the clear signs of hope within the United Methodist Church is "a widespread quest for personal spirituality and maturity. That's why questers are flocking to experiences such as Walk to Emmaus, Disciple Bible Study, Stephen Ministry, Bethel Bible, Promise Keepers, and small groups of all sorts."

Then too if anything positive and hopeful could be said about a loss of 42,000 members in 1997, it is that this number is less than the loss (49,000) in 1995 and 1996. Moreover, twenty-one of the Church's sixty-six conferences actually grew in membership. Maybe the "widespread quest for personal spirituality and maturity" that Bishop Owens referred to as reflected in increased attendance at Bible study and other spiritual growth groups is already beginning to bear tangible fruit.

Mission goals, primary objectives, inspiring resolutions, priority agendas, focus issues, it needs to be noted, on target though they might be, and to be sure a necessary and vital first step, do not in and of themselves bring about the transformational spiritual change and dynamic growth within the Church that we seek. By themselves, no matter how brilliantly written or well worded, they do not get the job done. If they did, in view of the voluminous sum of them that is presumably on record at virtually every level of United Methodism, we would certainly be one of the fastest growing Churches in the country. It is only when we seriously and sacrificially commit ourselves to implementing them, in deed more than word, in all areas and aspects of the Church's mission and ministry, primarily at the grassroots level of the local church, then we will experience true radical and inspirational transformation throughout the Church. Again, in the words of Christ Himself: "Why do you call Me, 'Lord, Lord' and do not do what I tell you?"

The phenomenal growth of Christianity that is spreading throughout the African continent is happening not because of the relevant resolutions and decisions made by the upper echelons of the Church. The proof and power of the faith lies in the doing, not simply in the knowing. Thus James emphasizes that the one who possesses the most convincing proof of true Christian discipleship is the one who is "a doer that acts" (James 1:25), and Paul in his letter to the Christians in Rome reinforces the same point (Rom. 2:13). And again in the words of Christ Himself: "Why do you call me Lord, Lord and do not do what I tell you?" (Luke 6:46)

In fact, Jesus ends His revolutionary Sermon on the Mount with this warning: "Everyone then who hears these words of mine and acts on them will be like a wise man who built his house on rock. The rain fell, the floods came, and the winds blew and beat on that house, but it did not fall, because it had been founded on rock. And everyone who hears these words of mine and does not act on them will be like a foolish man who built his house on sand. The rain fell, and the floods came, and the winds blew and beat against that house and it fell—and great was its fall!" (Matt. 7:24–27).

The phenomenal growth of Christianity that is spreading throughout the African continent is happening not because of the relevant resolutions and decisions made by the upper echelons of Church hierarchy and structure, but because rank and file members, as true and obedient disciples of Christ, faithfully commit themselves to do the will of the Lord as given in His Word enthusiastically, sacrificially, and joyfully as a matter of first priority.

Endnotes

Preface

1. *Boston Globe*, April 17, 1999.
2. *Methodism in Southern Africa* (Board of Global Ministries, UMC) SS 13 cm, April, 1995.
3. Ibid.

Chapter 1

1. *The United Methodist Review*, March 21, 1997.
2. *Wilson Quarterly*, Winter, 1997.
3. *Meditations on the Cross*, Dietrich Bonhoeffer.

Chapter 3

1. *Christianity Today*, August 15, 1994.

Chapter 4

1. *Challenge*, December 1998/January 1999.
2. *Challenge*, October/November 1998.
3. Ibid.
4. *Time*, March 30, 1998.
5. *Challenge*, December 1998/January 1999.
6. Ibid.

Chapter 5

1. *Newscope*, Vol. 26, No. 5, February 6, 1998.
2. *Newscope*, Vol. 26, No. 46, November 13, 1998.
3. *Newscope*, Vol. 26, No. 44, October 30, 1998.
4. *Newscope*, Vol. 27, No. 2, January 8, 1999.